THE AMERICAN SOUTH AS A POSTCOLONIAL SPACE:
THE SEARCH FOR IDENTITY IN WILLIAM FAULKNER'S WRITINGS

THE AMERICAN SOUTH AS A POSTCOLONIAL SPACE:
THE SEARCH FOR IDENTITY IN WILLIAM FAULKNER'S WRITINGS

A thesis submitted in partial fulfillment
of the requirements for the degree of
Master of Arts in English

By

Adam Long
Lyon College
Bachelor of Arts, 2006

May 2008
University of Arkansas

ABSTRACT

This paper explores the ways in which William Faulkner's writings share many of the concerns of postcolonial authors around the world, particularly focusing on the criticism of Edouard Glissant. In *Absalom, Absalom!*, *Light in August*, and *Go Down, Moses*, Faulkner's characters search for identity but fail in their searches because they are focused on establishing legitimacy. Despite the white aristocracy's failure to shift its focus from legitimacy, Faulkner's writings are full of alternative, nonlinear voices that act as counterpoint to the voices of Faulkner's protagonists.

TABLE OF CONTENTS

I. Introduction

William Faulkner frequently dealt with issues of race and class relations, creating

characters such as Joe Christmas, the protagonist of *Light in August*, a man both formed and

destroyed by racial conflict, internal and external. Despite the abundance of social criticism

already exploring this rich material, much work is yet to be done. Specifically, I propose that

a thorough postcolonial reading is helpful in bringing the complexity of Faulkner's

consideration of race and class into full relief. Even among the field of postcolonial readings

of Faulkner, most of the criticism has focused on black servants or poor whites as subaltern

characters[1]; almost no criticism has explored the way in which the rich whites of the South

function as a subaltern class in relation to the Northern forces that colonized the South during

Reconstruction. This silence is startling in light of both the Southern aristocracy's military

and economic defeat in the Civil War and its subsequent domination by the North, for as

Charles Baker argues, "Postcolonialism considers the process by which one culture

dominates another and the means through which the oppressed culture resists, thereby

reestablishing its own identity and autonomy" (3). I do not argue that the Southern

aristocracy was in as difficult a social or economic state as other subaltern groups in the

South. Nor do I argue that the Northern influence on the South was negative. Rather, I do

argue that in order to understand what is happening in the South during Reconstruction, it is

important to understand all aspects of the social hierarchy, even how ex-slaveholders are

adapting to a more modern world.

---

[1] For example, Richard Godden has a useful look into the way in which Caribbean islanders work as a subaltern class in much of Faulkner. See "Absalom, Absalom! *Haiti, and the Labor Industry: Reading Unreadable Revolutions." William Faulkner's Absalom, Absalom!: A Casebook. Ed. Fred Hobson. New York: Oxford UP, 2003. 251-82.*

Identifying the South as a postcolonial space is not an unproblematic premise, however, at least as far as the white aristocracy is concerned. Bill Ashcroft comments on the most common interpretation of a postcolonial culture, calling it "inevitably a hybridized phenomenon involving a dialectical relationship between the 'grafted' European cultural systems and an indigenous ontology, with its impulse to create or recreate an independent local identity" (195). Such an ontological difference between dominant and subaltern classes does clearly characterize the relationship between the white aristocracy and the Native American cultures, or even African Americans, though they have been forced from their native locality. White Southerners and Northerners are more similar, at least on the surface; they share the same language, some of the same basic institutions, and the same basic base of knowledge. Most importantly, both the South and the North are dominated by white landowners. Because of these surface similarities, some might argue that it would be impossible for the North to culturally dominate the South, as the cultures are interchangeable.

Such arguments assume an essential, diametrical opposition between the dominant and subaltern cultures in a postcolonial space. I would agree with Homi Bhabha that such a categorization is an oversimplification. Bhabha argues that colonialism necessarily results in what he calls "hybridity." M. Keith Booker connects this supposition with Bhabha's use of Derrida: "Central to Bhabha's critical project is a rather Derridean deconstruction of the opposition between the cultures of the colonizers and of the colonized. He thus insists that a complexly ambivalent cultural hybridity—on both sides—is the inevitable consequence of all colonial encounters" (157-8). Gayatri Chakravorty Spivak similarly argues for the complex relationship between dominant and subaltern cultures, saying "But one must nevertheless insist that the colonized subaltern *subject* is irretrievably heterogeneous" (79). As an example, she breaks down the complex layers of social hierarchy in postcolonial India.[2] Bart

Moore-Gilbert offers a perhaps more closely analogous example of the same concept: "The

example of Canada serves to suggest just how tangled and multi-faceted the term

'postcolonial' has now become in terms of its temporal, spatial, political and socio-cultural

meanings. Here there are at least five distinct but often overlapping contexts to which the

term might be applied" (10). On the one hand, the Canadian Anglo-Saxon upper class is

dominated politically by the United Kingdom and culturally by the omnipresent media of the

United States. At the same time, the Canadian upper class is dominant over the minority

francophone Quebecois and, perhaps even more strongly, over the indigenous peoples of the

region. Thus, the upper class Canadians are to some degree both subaltern and dominant. As

Spivak says, "The same class or element which was dominant in one area…could be among

the dominated in another" (79). This seems directly analogous to the white aristocracy of the

South during Faulkner's career, an aristocracy at the same time both subaltern in relationship

to the occupying North and dominant in relationship to blacks and poor whites.

The blurring of the lines between dominant and subaltern classes is a central point of

contention in postcolonial studies in general. Moore-Gilbert discusses many of the critiques

of postcolonial studies, particularly emphasizing the work of Aijaz Ahmad. Moore-Gilbert

summarizes, "Ahmad interprets postcolonial theory as the activity of a privileged and

deracinated class fraction, which is cut off from the material realities of 'Third Word'

struggles, the dynamic energies of which are appropriated and domesticated into a chic but

finally unchallenging intellectual commodity which circulates largely within the Western

academy" (18). The appropriation of postcolonial studies by the Western academy is key.

The academy determines the canon of texts to be studied, as well as the critical terminology

---

[2] For a chart breaking down the Indian social hierarchy, see Spivak 79.

with which to frame the debates within postcolonial studies. Postcolonial critics frequently use the works of Derrida and Foucault, among others, to understand the relationship between dominant and subaltern classes. Ahmad, at least in Moore-Gilbert's opinion, would argue that the necessity of using the language of dominant Western critics means that postcolonial studies have been "appropriated" by the academy.

The question, then, is not just whether Faulkner's own position as a member of the dominant class makes him incapable of ever truly acting as a member of a subaltern class; rather, the question is also whether Western critics can truly understand subaltern classes. Such doubts are valid, reminding critics of the complexity of texts and cautioning them against cultural arrogance. However, the fact that we may not ever be able to completely understand the heterogeneity that has resulted from colonialism should not preclude our desire to understand as much as we can. To this end, the postcolonial study of Faulkner presents some interesting opportunities. Not only does Faulkner exist in the middle of the heterogeneity that Spivak noted, viewing himself as both dominant and subaltern, but he also attempts to understand the classes which are subaltern in relation to him, the blacks and poor whites, and in doing so engages, however imperfectly, in the difficult work in which the academy is also engaged.

It is not necessary to view Faulkner as a completely postcolonial subject; in fact, it would be a mistake to understand him primarily as such. Nevertheless, postcolonial theory is useful as one tool for understanding Faulkner's work, especially since Faulkner clearly viewed himself as a product of cultural colonialism even though the vocabulary of postcolonial theory did not yet exist. Faulkner equates the Reconstruction South with both Scotland (under colonial English rule) and Japan (under United States control after World

War II). Of Japan, Joseph Blotner paraphrases Faulkner: "A hundred years ago, [Faulkner] began, the South had undergone a worse war and occupation than the Japanese had known. But now the whole country was stronger for this anguish. Young people in the South might then have asked the questions young Japanese were now asking about a hopeless future" (607-8). This connection between the South and Japan was not incidental, not solely based on the fact that each had lost a war; it was cultural, as well. Baker says, "Additionally, the two cultures had much in common: [Faulkner] noted that in Mississippi, 'there had been an aristocratic tradition like that of the samurai and there was, similarly, a peasantry'" (1). Baker continues, "[Faulkner] told the Japanese, 'I think that is why after our own disaster there rose in *my country, the South*, a resurgence of good writing'" (2). Not only do these comments reveal that Faulkner thought of his country as the South rather than as the United States, but it also reveals that he viewed that country as comparable to American-occupied Japan.

Similarly, Faulkner compared the Reconstruction South with the English-dominated Scotland. He says that "there was a kinship perhaps between the life of [Sir Walter] Scott's Highland and the life the Southerner led after Reconstruction. They too were in the aftermath of a land which had been conquered and devastated by people speaking its own language" (*FIU* 135). Such an attitude is apparent in Faulkner's novels, as well. In *Light in August*, Joanna Burden, the daughter of a carpetbagger never fully accepted by the local community, has an affair with Joe Christmas, a man of uncertain race and parentage. Referring to Burden, Faulkner calls the South "the place which was a *foreign land* to her and her people" (240, emphasis mine). The fact that Burden was born in the South does not change the fact she represents the dominant Northern culture: "She has lived in the house since she was born, yet she is still a stranger, a foreigner whose people moved in from the North during Reconstruction" (46). As far as Faulkner is concerned, the South is like a separate country, despite speaking the same language as the North. Further, it is a country which has been occupied by an invading army, much like Scotland or Japan.

Faulkner is not the first Southerner to describe the South this way. Baker discusses many of the policies of Reconstruction in terms of colonial policies worldwide, particularly focusing on the way in which these policies were received by the Southern white aristocracy.[3] He notes that the South was subject to a military rule: "To facilitate their compliance, the Reconstruction Act of 1866 divided the South into five military districts" (21). Baker compares such organization to the way in which the British Empire ruled areas such as India. In his opinion, "British rule in India, much like Northern rule in the South, was based on force if not on numbers" (16). Further, Baker notes that the regionalism of the North was similar to the imperialistic attitudes of England to Ireland: "The British considered all natives as Other and believed the Irish represented an inferior race, regardless of their pigmentation" (17). As a result of such imperialism, the white aristocracy of the South reacted very negatively to Reconstruction policies. Baker says, "In an intriguing move, some Southerners reacted to Northern colonization by proposing their own colonialism elsewhere, presumably to recreate their plantation society, complete with slaves, and thus perpetuate their own oppression of others rather than become oppressed themselves" (24). This last observation underscores my earlier assertion that the white aristocrats of the South were at the same time both dominant and subaltern.

Faulkner and many of his fellow Southern aristocrats, then, saw the Reconstruction South as a land occupied by a foreign power. The terms of postcolonial discourse recognize

---

[3] For a more complete discussion, see Baker, "Chapter One: The Essence of Empire." 11-29.

the complexity of such situations, allowing critics to understand subjects as belonging to both a dominant and a subaltern class and allowing critics to recognize the heterogeneity found both within and between postcolonial cultures without ignoring the fact that, despite the vast differences between these cultures and despite the various levels of occupation and oppression that led to them, there are still similarities which are worth investigating. As such, it is not surprising that postcolonial critics such as Edouard Glissant have chosen to explore the works of Faulkner. Glissant, especially in *Faulkner, Mississippi*, focuses on the way in which Faulkner deals with the black, Native American and Creole characters in his novels. These characters are clearly not part of the white aristocracy which I wish to discuss, belonging instead to an undeniably subaltern class. Despite the difference in Glissant's focus, his writings are useful as a departure point for my current project.

Specifically, Glissant posits that Faulkner's goal was never to assume the point of view of any class other than his own. Glissant says, "Faulkner may not come anywhere near these stereotypes, but neither does he render the 'real' situation of Blacks. Rather, he describes Blacks in a situation that suits his purpose. This is why their presence is so important: as a generalizing 'signified' (*signifié*), they embody a position (as people) that is weighty and substantial" (57). Faulkner thus does not attempt to describe the black perspective but rather focuses on the plight of the white aristocracy. Glissants suggests, "Perhaps he was convinced that the cry of revolt logically should come from Blacks and decided it was not up to him to sound it in turn" (63). Equally possible is that Faulkner sensed he was unable to portray the plight of the classes which his own class dominated.[4]

---

[4] Celia Britton suggests Faulkner's inability to portray blacks is a positive in that it is an acknowledgment of the complexity of cultural dominance. See *Edouard Glissant and Postcolonial Theory: Strategies of Language and Resistance.* Charlottesville, VA: U of Virginia P, 1999. 204.

My project, then, begins where Glissant's ends. Glissant explores the way in which Faulkner relates to the classes dominated by the Southern aristocracy. Looking at the black, creole, and Native American characters, he concludes that Faulkner does reveal much about race and class relations in the South, and even about the search for identity within the white aristocracy. I intend to expand from here, looking at the way in which the white aristocracy searches for identity in relation to Northern culture. This is not to say I will ignore the poor white, black, creole, and Native American characters in the novels. Rather, I will look at the way these characters add to the search for identity within the white aristocracy, a search which is sparked by the aristocracy's subaltern relationship to Northern culture.

I will begin by looking at *Absalom, Absalom!*. In this novel, the identity crisis focuses on Quentin Compson, a Southerner studying at Harvard. Quentin is called upon to recreate the story of Thomas Sutpen, a man who moved to Mississippi and created a successful plantation, only to see his plantation and family destroyed during the Civil War. Quentin's search to understand the fall of Sutpen becomes his search to understand the defeat of the South. Thus, through exploring Sutpen, he is exploring his own identity. In order to do this, he (with the help of many of the other characters in the novel) must create details and explanations, including creating the life story of a creole named Charles Bon, through whom Quentin begins to live vicariously. The story is not linear. Rather, it flows in and out, playing scenes over and over and deferring key facts and suppositions until the end. I will explore this method of storytelling, looking at Glissant's comments on Faulkner's storytelling. Particularly, I will look at the way in which the "deferred revelation" of the central scene defies the Hegelian concept of History in favor of what Barbara Ladd calls a "creole poetics." Despite Quentin's attempts to find an identity apart from the Western ideology of History, his concerns about legitimacy confound his efforts; he commits suicide a few months after his final relation of the Sutpen narrative.

I will next consider the ways in which *Light in August* negotiates the conflict between legitimacy and identity, for as Glissant suggests, the search for legitimacy often prevents the successful negotiation of the search for identity. In *Light in August*, two characters, whose paths only incidentally cross, are searching for identity. Joe Christmas is of uncertain racial heritage and must determine how to live in a society defined by racial identity when he does not have one himself. Gail Hightower, while not having the racial conflicts of Christmas, is also an outsider in the town, his fantasies about his grandfather in the Civil War having drowned out his interactions with reality. The novel juxtaposes these two characters with Lena Grove, a character who seems free of worries about legitimacy and who perhaps presents a solution to such concerns.

Finally, I will explore the solution more thoroughly by looking at *Go Down, Moses*, a novel which combines the plights of white aristocrats, Native Americans, and blacks. This novel explores tales of genesis, abandoning the dominant Western myths in favor of atavistic cultural priorities. Specifically, the novel features several characters who have metaphorically birthed themselves, thus freeing themselves from class by freeing themselves from society. These characters are juxtaposed with Ike McCaslin, a white aristocrat acutely aware of his dual role as dominant and subaltern. In the end, Ike unsuccessfully tries to free himself in the same way as these other characters, repudiating his land and birthright. His solution proves unrealistic, however, since it ignores the responsibility he has to try to cause real change in society. Despite this, the voices of the Native Americans, blacks, and women serve as counterpoint to Ike's crisis, again presenting the readers with a nonlinear narrative that resists the dominant view of History. These three novels, then, work together to explore the difference between the search for legitimacy, as characterized by Western patrilineal ideals, and the search for identity sought for in a genuine "creole poetics."

II. 'Deferred Revelation' and the 'creole poetics' of *Absalom, Absalom!*

My discussion of *Absalom, Absalom!* is essentially a case study in the way in which a

Southern white aristocrat negotiates the identity crisis that comes from the schizophrenia

created by his duel role as subaltern and dominant, as well as the way in which this

negotiation is thwarted by the dominant ideological system. In looking at the character of

Quentin Compson, I will follow Ladd's premise: "Under the circumstances Faulkner's

decision to embed the truth in the drama of performance, to bind information so tightly to

interpretation, leads the reader to ask not only who or what Charles Bon was—whether he

was black or white, possible son or would-be husband—but to ask who and what the

speakers are with respect to the Charles Bon they construct" ("Direction" 233). Similarly, I

will look less at the facts surrounding the life of Thomas Sutpen and more at what the readers

can assume about Quentin Compson based on the Sutpen he creates. Ladd and I will come to

somewhat different conclusions, however. Ladd suggests Quentin's failure is his inability to

develop a future (in the sense of a Hegelian vision of History[5] in a colonial setting driven by

"creole poetics"[6]). She says, "Quentin and Shreve (like the other speakers in the novel) fail

to the extent that they fail to rewrite the old stories in a way that provides Quentin with a

future" ("Poetics" 35). In other words, Ladd understands Quentin's attempt at "synthesis" to

be doomed by American realities (35). On the contrary, I believe Quentin's failure comes

from his inability to recognize the need to develop a "creole poetics." Instead, he sees a

---

[5] For a full discussion of Hegel's view of History as it relates to *Absalom, Absalom!* see *Barbara Ladd.
"Faulkner Glissant, and Creole Poetics." Faulkner in the Twenty-First Century: Faulkner and
Yoknapatawpha, 2000. Ed. Robert Hamblin and Ann J. Abadie. Jackson, MS: UP of Mississippi, 2003. 31-49.*
[6] Ladd defines "creole poetics": "A creole poetics is defined in terms of simultaneity rather than chronology or
succession, in terms of irruption rather than development, in terms of exile and return rather than origin and
departure" ("Poetics" 34).

picture of what he could become in the future and tries to use logical rules of causality to envision a way in which he might be able to alter his fate.

Fundamental to the understanding of Quentin's focus on the causality of history is recognition of the centrality of the events at Sutpen's Hundred as a dramatic turning point for Quentin. In terms of the form of the novel, Quentin's experiences at Sutpen's Hundred are the delayed climax. Glissant calls this a "deferred revelation," saying, "it is an accumulating mystery and a whirling vertigo—gathering momentum rather than being resolved, through deferral and disclosure—and centered in a place to which he felt a need to give meaning" (9). Such a "whirling vertigo" resists a linear narrative, inviting instead the sort of poetics which Quentin needs. In this case, the "deferred revelation" begins when Rosa calls Quentin to her house and begins telling him the story of Sutpen. Mr. Compson then corrects and amends her story on the porch of the Compson house the evening before Quentin is to accompany Rosa out to Sutpen's Hundred to see who is hiding there. Then there is a lapse of time. Quentin is at Harvard, and Mr. Compson's letter about Rosa's funeral has prompted him to retell the story to his roommate Shreve. This shift in narration is significant. The story that Quentin tells Shreve is different from the one he learned from Rosa and his father. He claims he learned something at Sutpen's Hundred. Shreve notices Quentin's story does not match with Mr. Compson's: "He seems to have got an awful lot of delayed information awful quick, after having waited forty-five years. If he knew all this, what was his reason for telling you that the trouble between Henry and Bon was the octoroon woman?" (214). Quentin replies that Mr. Compson "didn't know it then," because Quentin is the one who told Mr. Compson after returning from Sutpen's Hundred: "I did [tell him…] The day after we—

after that night when we—" (214). The events at Sutpen's Hundred cause Quentin to recast the character of Thomas Sutpen.

It seems unlikely however that Quentin learns anything factual at Sutpen's Hundred. Quentin does see and talk to Henry Sutpen, yet there is no reason to believe that anything substantive came from that conversation. After all, the circular nature of the conversation suggests Faulkner intended the text of the conversation given to be the complete conversation, and Henry does little in the conversation but identify himself to Quentin (298). Quentin's own reaction to the situation confirms this reading: "He could not help it. He was twenty years old; he was not afraid, because what he had seen out there could not harm him, yet he ran" (297). Quentin is aware that his response is incongruous with the facts of the meeting. Based on the facts, he should not be afraid, yet he is. His response is emotional and not rational; he is affected by what he *saw*, not by what he heard.

I argue that what Quentin sees in that room is his own future, or at least the future he fears will be his. He sees the waste of a man, "the heir, the apparent (though not obvious)" of a Southern family, who has repudiated his responsibility (296). The details of the description of Henry in the bed are filled with images of waste: "the yellow sheets and pillow, the wasted yellow face with closed, almost transparent eyelids on the pillow, the wasted hands crossed on the breast as if he were already a corpse" (298). Quentin is also the heir apparent of a Southern family. He, too, is incapable of fulfilling his familial responsibilities; *The Sound and the Fury* portrays him as being incapable of fulfilling his obligation (as he sees it) to protect his sister, possibly because of his incestuous desire. Quentin, like Henry, will ultimately abdicate his responsibility, Quentin by committing suicide. *Absalom* occurs before this complete abdication, however; Quentin relates his story to Shreve some three or four months before his suicide. Yet the image of Henry still resonates with him. The story of Sutpen Quentin tells is altered by the resonant image of a wasted man who has repudiated his responsibility. This parallels the situation of the postcolonial South. It has seen its own doom in its defeat in the Civil War, and it is left to come to terms with its past by coming up with a cogent narrative to explain its loss. In this way, Quentin's search for identity in light of his realization of his possible wasted existence is a picture of the concerns of his class.

The way in which this image changes Quentin can be seen in the change in the characterization of Thomas Sutpen from Mr. Compson's story to Quentin's.[7] Rather than blaming Sutpen for the downfall of Sutpen's Hundred, Mr. Compson allows for the possibility that Sutpen is a victim. He explains Rosa's description of Sutpen's evil as being a product of her preconceived notions: "she was doubtless one of that league of Jefferson women who on the second day after the town saw him five years ago, had agreed never to forgive him for not having any past, and who had remained consistent" (40). Further, he explains the flaws in the relationship between Sutpen and Henry as logically following from the natural relationship between father and son. He describes Henry's stubborn thinking after learning of Bon's morganastic ceremony, having Henry think "*I will believe; I will. I will. Even if it is so, even if what my father told me is true and which, in spite of myself, I cannot keep from knowing is true, I will still believe*" (72). For Mr. Compson, Sutpen is a wise and misunderstood father, trying to save his son from his own self-deceit.

Not only does Mr. Compson not portray Sutpen as a villain, but he also does not blame any other character. Henry's rebellion against his father is a natural part of

---

[7] I do not want to oversimplify the narration by dividing it neatly into two sections. The text is far more complex than this, having as narrators also Rosa and Shreve, among other complexities. My purpose in the simple contrast is to observe some aspects of Quentin's narration. Clearly, a study of the way in which Quentin interacts with the other layers of the narration would reveal other aspects of Quentin's character.

maturation. Mr. Compson calls Sutpen "the father who is the natural enemy of any son" (83). The condition is portrayed as universal. In fact, in all areas but that of standing up for the honor of his sister, Mr. Compson sees Henry as heroic, even having him rescue Bon from the battlefield. Henry is "the private who carried that officer [Bon], shot through the shoulder, on his back while the regiment fell back under the Yankee guns at Pittsburg Landing" (98). He rescues Bon while under fire, even if such a rescue ignores his central responsibility of protecting his family. This is not the only time Mr. Compson does not blame a character for the repudiation of a central responsibility. He introduces Goodhue Coldfield as "that man who was later to nail himself in his attic and starve to death rather than look upon his native land in the throes of repelling an invading army" (47). Yet Mr. Compson does not condemn Coldfield for not defending the South. He explains, "But he was not a coward, even though his conscience may have objected, as your grandfather said, not so much to the idea of pouring out human blood and life, but at the idea of waste: of wearing out and eating up and shooting away material in any cause whatever" (65). Though Mr. Compson acknowledges some flaws in the characters in his narration, he is unwilling to attribute any guilt to them for the fall of the South.

In Mr. Compson's narration, the South seems to take on the form of Mr. Compson's Bon, a victim awaiting a fate that cannot be overthrown. Mr. Compson calls Bon "the fatalist" and pictures him as patiently awaiting Henry's making a decision (97). For him, the death of Bon is predetermined: "that afternoon four years later should have happened the next day, the four years, the interval, mere anti climax" (94). It is important that Mr. Compson compares Bon's fate with that of the United States. He says:

> [...] an attenuation and prolongation of a conclusion already ripe to happen, by the War, by a stupid and bloody aberration in the high (and impossible)

> destiny of the United States, maybe instigated by that family fatality which
> possessed, along with all circumstance, that *curious lack of economy between
> cause and effect* which is always a characteristic of fate when reduced to using
> human beings for tools, material. (94, italics mine)

Bon is fated to die, the South is fated to fall, and neither Henry's nor Coldfield's inaction nor

the actions of Bon and Sutpen can change this.

In his narration to Shreve, Quentin rejects his father's fatalism. Against a

postcolonial landscape, this is not surprising. Baker describes the generational differences

frequently found in reactions to colonization and how these generational differences apply to

the Reconstruction South: "Stinging from their military defeat and the ensuing attitude of the

victorious North, the vanquished Southerners first reacted with shame and repudiated their

past; later, they returned to their history, like postcolonial authors worldwide, to recapture the

essence of their culture" (47). In this case, Quentin rejects the belief the South was doomed

by fate, largely because he does not want to believe he is doomed by fate. He does not want

to see himself lying in a bed, a wasted shadow of his former self, having repudiated his

responsibility. Rather, he seeks a narrative, a causality, which would have prevented

Sutpen's downfall, hoping to find a causality to escape his own. In the end, however, his

insistence on strict causality to provide him with legitimacy ultimately denies him the future

it seemed to promise.

It is, of course, impossible to determine if Quentin is more or less factually accurate

about the details of Sutpen's life than is Mr. Compson. It is also irrelevant. Quentin may

have done an excellent job figuring out what must have gone on, or his story may be grossly

inaccurate. Either way, Quentin clearly projects his search for causality onto his version of

the Sutpen story. When he retells what Sutpen told his grandfather, he has his grandfather

insist that Sutpen proceed "with at least some regard for cause and effect even if none for logical sequence and continuity" (199). Quentin does not succumb to Sutpen's weakness in

storytelling, creating a strong sense of causality. No image captures this more clearly than

the moral ledger which Quentin envisions. Quentin says it is "as if nature held a balance and

kept a book and offered a recompense for the torn limbs and outraged hearts even if man did

not" (202). Similarly, he imagines Sutpen comparing life to the rules of baking. Quentin

imagines Sutpen having "that innocence which believed that the ingredients of morality were

like the ingredients of pie or cake and once you had measured them and balanced them and

mixed them and put them into the oven it was all finished and nothing but pie or cake could

come out" (211-2). Importantly, Quentin applies causality to society as well as to Sutpen's

understanding. Quentin says, "the South would realize that it was now paying the price for

having erected its economic edifice not on the rock of stern morality but on the shifting sands

of opportunism and moral brigandage" (209). For Quentin, every moral decision has a price,

a consequence.

Besides superimposing a desire for causality onto Sutpen's character, Quentin also

tries to solve the mystery of what happened between Henry and Bon by relying on cause and

effect. In order to do this, Quentin (with Shreve's help) creates the character of the New

Orleans lawyer. This lawyer literally keeps a moral ledger, constantly tracking the net worth

of Sutpen: *"Today he finished robbing a drunken Indian of a hundred miles of virgin land,*

val. 25,000. At 2:31 today came up out of swamp with final plank for house. val. in conj.

with land 40,000. 7:52 p.m. today married. Bigamy threat val. minus nil. unless quick

buyer" (241). Quentin and Shreve imagine the lawyer keeping up with the details of

Sutpen's life as a part of a larger design, a design to get Sutpen's money, which required intricate planning, such as insuring that Bon meet Henry at the University of Mississippi.

Quentin insists that Bon knew

> that the lawyer was up to something and though he knew that was just money, yet he knew that within his (the lawyer's) known masculine limitations he (the lawyer) could be almost as dangerous as the unknown quantity which was his mother; and no this—school, college—and he twenty-eight years old. And not only that, but this particular college, which he had never heard of, which ten years ago did not even exist; and knowing too that it was the lawyer who had chosen it for him. (250)

The lawyer's design comes to fruition when he eventually steals Bon's money. Following Quentin's logic, Shreve interjects, "so without doubt the lawyer had murdered her [Bon's mother] before he stole the money" (271). This murder serves as a logical ending to the story of the lawyer, but like the rest of the lawyer's details, it is a product of Quentin and Shreve's imagination, Shreve borrowing largely from the imagery and logic with which Quentin overlaid the story. The lawyer *must* have existed. Otherwise, the story would not *make sense*.

The actions of the lawyer do not explain everything that transpired between Henry and Bon, however, so Quentin and Shreve are forced to change the story once again, trying to create a cause that explains Henry's murder of Bon. In this account, Bon is not a fatalist: "Bon whom Mr Compson had called a fatalist but who, according to Shreve and Quentin, did not resist Henry's dictum and design for the reason that he neither knew nor cared what Henry intended to do because he had long since realized that he did not know yet what he himself was going to do" (268). Bon eventually decides to try to get Sutpen to acknowledge him as a son. He asks for Henry's permission to marry Judith, saying "He has never acknowledged me. He just warned me. You are the brother and the son. Do I have your permission, Henry?" (279). Bon's desire, then, is not so much for revenge, but to be recognized by his father. That is why he came to Sutpen's Hundred in the first place, that is why he was willing to wait until Henry made up his mind, and that is what he has failed to achieve when finally he asks Henry for Judith's hand.[8]

But this is not good enough for Quentin (and Shreve) either. An illegitimate son is not cause enough for fratricide. Quentin and Shreve search for something more extreme which could have caused the murder. Shreve suggests incest, and Quentin goes silent, presumably thinking about his own anxieties about his relationship with his sister.[9] Shreve says, "That's right. Dont say it. Because I would know you are lying" (260). When Shreve changes the subject from incest, Quentin joins back in, eventually deciding that the crime was something greater than incest. He has Bon say to Henry, "*So it's the miscegenation, not the incest, which you cant bear*" (285). In the same conversation, Bon drives the point home, saying "*No I'm not [your brother]. I'm the nigger that's going to sleep with your sister. Unless you stop me, Henry*" (286). Quentin has found an absolute and compelling cause behind the fratricide, a cause other than incest. All the details (if not the facts) of the story now line up, following the rules of cause and effect.

Quentin's application of causality to the story of Sutpen does not help him cope with the image of Henry, however. At novel's end he is immobile, lying in his bed, no different from the night he returned from Sutpen's Hundred. On the other hand, Shreve is satisfied, released from the story. He says, "Which is all right, it's fine; it clears the whole ledger" (302). But Quentin lies motionless in bed. His storytelling has not released him. If Quentin is trying to reclaim his past, if he is trying to come to terms with his subaltern status by

---

[8] Ladd sums up this version of Bon nicely: "the hubris of an American innocent, Thomas Sutpen, creates a retributive agent in the figure of Charles Bon" ("Direction" 231). I would only add the phrase "according to Quentin and Shreve."

[9] For more detail on the way in which Quentin relates to the theme of incest, see *Karl F. Zender. "Faulkner and the Politics of Incest." American Literature 70.4 (1998): 739-65.*

developing an identity, why does he fail? How is Quentin different from the subaltern

characters of other authors? I believe the answer lies in what Quentin's narration reveals

about his character. While he is willing to try to reform the past, he is only willing to do so

using the rules of the dominant ideology, the rules of cause and effect, the rules which result

in his destruction.

Quentin's inability to move past the causality he has created is emphasized in the way

Quentin's narration invites the readers to compare his experience with that of Sutpen. Both

characters' formative experiences involved being stopped outside a door. In Quentin's

narration, Sutpen tells Grandfather Compson how he was turned away from the door of a

Tidewater plantation: "He had been told to go around to the back door even before he could

state his errand, who had sprung from a people whose houses didn't have back doors [...] In

fact, he had actually come on business, in the good faith of business which he had believed

that all men accepted" (188). This door is never mentioned before Quentin goes to Sutpen's

Hundred, yet Quentin imagines this experience as central to Sutpen's character development.

Similarly, Quentin struggles to cross a threshold, the door to Henry's bedroom at Sutpen's

Hundred. When he finally does enter the door, the image of the wasted Henry paralyzes him

with fear. The door is also a mental barrier which Quentin cannot pass:

> [H]e had something which he still was unable to pass: that door, that gaunt
> tragic dramatic self-hypnotised youthful face like the tragedian in a college
> play, an academic Hamlet waked from some trancement of the curtain's
> falling and blundering across the dusty stage from which the rest of the cast
> had departed last commencement, the sister facing him across the wedding
> dress which she was not to use, not even to finish. (142)

Behind Quentin's mental block, then, is the image of a sister facing marriage and the image

of the wasted Henry which Quentin will become if he cannot come to terms with his

relationship to his sister. Whereas Sutpen's design in building his plantation is to create a world in which he can pass his door, in which he will be in charge, Quentin's design in recreating the Sutpen myth is an attempt to cross his own threshold, to come to terms with his past, particularly his relationship with his sister, a relationship marked by his inability to protect her virginity, at best, or his desire to take her virginity, at worst. Both are, in essence, threats to legitimacy. As Glissant says, "More significantly than any appropriation, incest is the absolute abandonment of legitimacy" (129). Just as Sutpen sought legitimacy through the creation of his plantation, Quentin is searching for legitimacy by creating a pure bloodline.

Both Quentin's and Sutpen's designs are attempts to escape their subaltern class. For Sutpen, this involves trying to change his class from the subaltern poor white to the dominant Southern aristocracy. In the Tidewater, "He had learned the difference not only between white men and black ones, but he was learning that there was a difference between white men and white men not to be measured by lifting anvils or gouging eyes or how much whskey you could drink then get up and walk out of the room" (183). This realization leads to Sutpen's desire to become a part of the dominant class of white men. As Quentin tells it, however, part of Sutpen's motivation is an obligation to the past to fulfill this social transition: "All of a sudden he [Sutpen] discovered, not what he wanted to do but what he just had to do, had to do it whether he wanted to or not, because if he did not do it he knew that he could never live with himself for the rest of his life, never live with what all the men and women that had died to make him had left inside of him for him to pass on" (178). For Quentin, Sutpen's impetus is an obligation both to himself and to his forbears to become a part of the dominant social group.

Quentin feels a similar impetus. He feels obligated to come to terms with the loss of the South in the Civil War, a search which becomes the vessel for his more personal search.

The novel starts with Rosa calling Quentin to her house, expecting him to write down the story of Thomas Sutpen, to come to terms with it.[10] As the story begins to consume Quentin, he thinks, "*I shall have to never listen to anything else but this again forever so apparently not only a man never outlives his father but not even his friends and acquaintances do*" (222). Shreve explains the same concept:

> We [Canadians] dont live among defeated grandfathers and freed slaves (or have I got it backward and was it your folks that are free and the niggers that lost?) and bullets in the dining room table and such, to be always reminding us to never forget. What is that? something you live and breathe in like air? a kind of vacuum filled with wraithlike and indomitable anger and pride and glory and in happenings that occurred and ceased fifty years ago? a kind of entailed birthright father and son and father and son of never forgiving General Sherman, so that forever more as long as your children's children produce children you wont be anything but a descendant of a long line of colonels killed in Pickett's charge at Manassas? (289)

Quentin's heritage insists that he continue fighting the Civil War, that he continue to fight against the dominant North. Like his version of Sutpen, Quentin is resisting being subaltern, searching instead for the dominance which the end of slavery took away. While Sutpen resisted physically by building a plantation, Quentin resists by building a narrative that promises to let him surpass defeat.[11]

If Quentin and Sutpen have a similar design in mind, it is not surprising that their designs meet a similar end. Sutpen's Hundred burns to the ground, and Quentin commits suicide, no longer able to handle the burden of the past. Both ultimately remain subaltern. This is not because they fail in their design, however, but because they stick to their design too unrelentingly. As Ramón Saldívar says, "the real threat to Sutpen's 'design' is the very plantation itself (and the plantation system) that is the object of his desires" (101). For

---

[10] Baker suggests that Rosa is intentionally building upon the trend of the Southern Renaissance. See Ch. 2 for a full discussion of the Southern Renaissance and how it relates to Quentin.

[11] For a discussion of how the Irish resisted with culture rather than with violence, see Baker 36-7.

Quentin's Sutpen, this comes from his inability to recognize that others do not strictly follow the rules which they profess. He comes to a moment of crisis where he can have everything he wants, except he will have to break one of his rules in such a way that no one will ever know. He says:

> [E]ither I destroy my design with my own hand, which will happen if I am forced to play my last trump card, or do nothing, let matters take the course which I know they will take and see my design complete itself quite normally and naturally and successfully to the public eye, yet to my own in such a fashion as to be a mockery and a betrayal of that little boy who approached that door fifty years ago and was turned away. (220)

Sutpen is so focused on his design that he will not waver from it, no matter the circumstances of the real world. Further, he will never question the morality of the dominant culture, the plantation system, instead accepting the societal hierarchy as an amoral given. He says, "You see I had a design in my mind. Whether it was good or a bad design is beside the point; the question is, Where did I make the mistake in it" (212).

Quentin makes a similar mistake. He will not yield from a cause and effect narrative in order to deal with reality. In terms of postcolonial theory, he cannot get past the Hegelian logic of the dominant class, the logic that shows him that the effect is always going to be his ending up like Henry. As Baker says, "anti-imperialists wish to reclaim control of their past and no longer be defined by others, so they must intentionally subvert the assumptions of the metrolpole" (47). Further, Ladd would suggest that the assumptions of the metropole are the assumptions of Hegelian causality: "It is important to emphasize that Sutpen's is not in any way a design of his own invention. It is a recapitulation of the design implicit in Western History" ("Poetics" 36). These assumptions are what Quentin does not subvert. He seems to avoid looking past causality, because doing so would require him to confront his anxieties about his sister. Even while being concerned about cause and effect, he is unwilling to discuss a scenario involving incest. This is his hang-up. He cannot confront the truth that legitimacy is less important than identity, and so relies on the facts, just as Sutpen was too "innocent" to confront the truth that the plantation system was unjust and no number of rules could change that. What Quentin says of Sutpen's logic applies to his own: "And he not calling it retribution, no sins of the father come home to roost; not even calling it bad luck, but just a mistake: that mistake which he could not discover himself" (215). Such oversimplifying of a narrative works neither for Sutpen nor for Quentin.

Through his narration of the Sutpen story, Quentin reveals to the readers that he sees much of Sutpen in himself, and like Sutpen, his design is doomed to fail because he is unwilling to see the fluidity within the story. His flaw is not that he cannot envision a future, as Ladd suggests. Rather, his flaw is that he refuses to adapt what she calls a "creole poetics," opting instead for the causality of the dominant class's narration. Though Quentin is unable to find a non-linear narration, Faulkner importantly does. His "deferred revelation" of the events at Sutpen's Hundred is like the wisteria blooming outside of Rosa's house, winding in and out, going back and forth but gradually upward in a nonlinear growth. This anticipates the techniques Faulkner uses in later novels, some of which are discussed below.

III. The Search for Legitimacy in *Light in August*

Light in August addresses many of the same themes as *Absalom, Absalom!*, particularly exploring the South's search for identity in the aftermath of the Civil War. While the main action of the novel takes place after the end of Reconstruction, the effects of Reconstruction are everywhere, most notably in the character of Joanna Burden, the daughter of a carpetbagger, "still a stranger, a foreigner" (46). Similarly, the former pastor Gail Hightower has never been able to escape from the legacy of the Civil War. He, too, has been branded an outsider by the local populace, being unable to live in the present because of his obsession with the War, "being born about thirty years after the only day he seemed to have ever lived in—that day when his grandfather was shot from the galloping horse" (62). The stories of these two characters unfold beside that of Joe Christmas. Joanna becomes Joe's lover; Hightower only meets Joe in an instant at the end of the novel. Yet the ideology shaping these characters is the force which prevents Joe from acculturating himself to society.

The past remains central in *Light in August*. Joseph W. Reed focuses on the importance of time in the novel: "an unremembered action, an answer, a word deep in the past can prove to be the root cause of a complex response or violent action erupting in the present" (69). Joe's present actions are determined by the complexities of the past, just as Quentin's fate was tied inextricably to the events at Sutpen's Hundred. Reed further argues, "Here the past is central: individual freedom or compulsion is primarily determined by a character's success or failure in dealing with his past" (64). Again like Quentin, Joe's challenge is to come to terms with the past and negotiate a present identity free from an imprisoning ideology. In terms of a larger social question, *August*, like *Absalom*, seeks to negotiate the occupation of the North and develop an identity for subaltern Southerners.

Light in August is no mere re-telling of *Absalom*, however. Rather, it raises many important issues, only hinted at in *Absalom*, that enrich a postcolonial reading of Faulkner. Joe Christmas is especially interesting in that he has no memory of his past. He is abandoned at an orphanage on Christmas (hence, the name). He does not know who his parents were or their racial history. Physically, his complexion is roughly Mediterranean, and some of the citizens of Jefferson say he looks Italian. Such slightly dark skin raises the possibility Joe is an octoroon, though there is no evidence to support this. As Judith Bryant Wittenberg says, "It is striking—and may seem paradoxical—that the Faulkner novel most centrally concerned with an issue that suffused so much of his corpus contains not a single significant character who is identifiably African-American" (146). Joe has no past; he only has a *possible* past, one formed in his attempt to find legitimacy.

Importantly, the ideology leading to Joe's desire for legitimacy is not just a matter of racial biases. If that were the case, the Southern and Northern ideologies would very possibly be inseparable. Indeed, such racial biases exist in the novel and in the post-bellum South, and a reading focused on this aspect of Southern ideology, and how Joe (as a possible black man) is subaltern in relation to it, would likely yield very useful results. Such a focus would stray from my purpose, however, which is to explore the way in which the white aristocracy of the South is subaltern in relation to the Northern ideology. As such, my reading will focus largely on the way Joe (as an apparently white man) is influenced by the most prevalent and most decidedly Northern ideology in the novel, the New England

Puritanism[12] espoused by many of the characters. In doing so, I will explore many of the other white characters in the novel, especially Hightower.[13]

Even in terms of the relationship between white characters, the dominant ideology is not exclusively Northern. Certainly, the plantation system was founded on dominance and relied heavily on a belief in patrilineal legitimacy to justify the continuation of the system. Despite this, Reconstruction does cause a new focus on legitimacy. By ending slavery and occupying the South, the North has removed the Southerners from their dominant positions, taking away their identity. To this end, the North did not create the ideology dominant in the South during Reconstruction, though it did contribute to the necessity of the South being no longer able to define itself in terms of the ideology. Further, for reasons I will discuss below, Faulkner describes this ideology in Northern terms, even in instances when the basis of the ideology is really Southern.

As in *Absalom*, the dominant ideology prevents the main characters from developing an independent identity. In terms of the white Southern aristocracy, Glissant suggests the dominant ideology forces the characters to strive for a legitimacy which is impossible to establish. Of Sam Fathers (whom I will explore in depth in my discussion of *Go Down, Moses*), Glissant says, "His actions cast a bad light on legitimacy, which is the guarantee of all stability, and then on family lineage, the visible envelope of legitimacy. This is the whole story of the tragedy of the county" (74). Such legitimacy is what Joe and Hightower are

---

[12] For a full discussion of Faulkner and Puritanism, see *Walter Taylor. Faulkner's Search for a South. Urbana: U of Illinois P, 1983.*

[13] Alliyah I. Abdur-Rahman addresses the frequently-made postulation that Hightower is a closeted gay man, tying his homosexuality to Joe's lack of racial identity: "I attend specifically to Faulkner's linking of racial ambiguity and homoeroticism in the figure of Joe Christmas, arguing that Faulkner uses the historical fact of miscegenation and the perceived failure of white masculinity to critique Southern culture and history and to offer ways of revamping and reconstituting whiteness in the modern—meaning postslavery—moment" (177). See *"White Disavowal, Black Enfranchisement, and the Homoerotic in William Faulkner's Light in August." The Faulkner Journal 22 (2007): 176-92.*

looking for, and what their religious training teaches them they ought to be looking for. This is not true of Lena Grove, however, the wandering pregnant woman whose story is the frame to the novel. She cares nothing about legitimacy; her impending birth of a bastard child is a constant reminder. In Glissant's opinion, a character such as hers is more connected to the way Faulkner portrays blacks: "They do not play with the devil or damn themselves in order to establish a domain; they do not kill merely to safeguard their filial ties" (60). Lena has an individual identity even in the midst of the dominant ideology.

In order to fully understand the importance of Lena, it is important to first see the way in which Puritan ideology has shaped the characters with whom Lena interacts. Indeed, the very supposition that religion in the novel is Puritan is problematic. Certainly, the South has many fundamentalist groups of its own, many of which have only the most cursory connection historically to Puritanism. A character such as Simon McEachern could be seen to follow the example of someone such as John Knox (a decidedly old-world figure) rather than someone such as Jonathan Edwards. Despite this, all of the religion in the novel is conflated, the structure of the flashbacks forcing the readers to understand Joe's final relationship with Joanna as being an outgrowth from his earlier relationships and the juxtaposition of key scenes making the religion of the various characters (except perhaps Hightower) interchangeable. Further, the only concrete labels that Faulkner attaches to this conflated religion identify it as New England Puritanism. As such, I will use this simplified term throughout, recognizing that such a conflation is important in understanding Joe, Joe's past being stripped away with his identity in much the same way the South can only be understood in terms of the North.

Joe, then, represents both the identity crisis that comes from having identity stripped away and the futility of trying to create identity by attempting to restore a legitimacy that never existed, a technique clearly couched by Faulkner in Northern terms. As such, it is necessary not only to see how Joe is dominated, but also to understand how all the influences on Joe's life are understood through Joe's relationship with Joanna. Joe's earliest memories are of his grandfather, Doc Hines. Hines is a ranting fundamentalist preacher who takes the pulpit to espouse his supremacist views. Hines murders Joe's mother and then follows him to the orphanage to ensure that Joe's lack of identity is complete. Thus, Hines is the first person who indoctrinates Joe. Even though Joe is very young at the time, the parallels between Joe's behavior in later life and that of Hines suggests Hines is successful in teaching his ideology to Joe.

Hines's first major influence on Joe is his killing of Milly, Joe's mother. When Hines learns Milly has been impregnated by a man from the circus, he concludes, "My wife has bore me a whore" (377). Milly believes the man from the circus is Mexican, and there is no evidence to contradict her. Yet Hines, probably because of his preconceived racial categories, claims he knows the man is black. As such, he kills the man, and then refuses to get Milly medical help, causing her to die in childbirth. In fact, "he stood outside the hall door where he could see Milly until she died" (379). Then, he takes the child Joe and abandons him on the front step of the orphanage, saying to his wife, "He is dead to you and to me and to God and to all God's world forever and ever more" (382). Thus, Hines is responsible for Joe's physical abandonment.

This behavior has more than just physical implications. By stripping Joe of his racial identity, Hines also ensures that Joe's abandonment has ideological implications. Joe clearly wants to know what his racial heritage is. As a child at the orphanage, he tries to understand racial differences, going as far as following around a black gardener, finally asking, "How come you are a nigger?" (383). The man answers, "You are worse than that. You don't know what you are. And more than that, you wont never know. You'll live and you'll die and you wont never know" (384). This is the curse which Hines ensures Joe suffers from; Hines says, "I have put the mark on him and now I am going to put the knowledge" (371). Laura Doyle argues Hines "kill[s] Joe's parents [again] by marring his identity" (341). This lack of racial knowledge is a curse, because Joe lives in a society in which racial heritage is critical to identity. As Joe explains to the gardener, "God aint no nigger" (384). The gardener replies, "I reckon you ought to know what God is, because don't nobody but God know what you is" (384). Because of Joe's lack of race in a society in which ideologically he is told whites are closer to God, he is forced to seek racial identity so he can be worthwhile. As Walter Taylor says, "Doc had bequeathed Joe another legacy: he had shackled him to a social identity marked out in American society as that of a scapegoat" (68).[14] Further, Joe's society insists identity is tied to legitimacy of birth; it is Joe's illegitimacy more than anything which Hines seems to hate. Since Joe's birth (and thus race) are ambiguous, Joe can never have an identity so long as the identity is necessarily founded on patrilineal legitimacy.

Hines not only curses Joe with racial ambiguity, but he also instills in Joe a strong sense of racial hatred. Hines's racial hatred is most clearly seen when he takes the pulpit:

> [...] this white man who very nearly depended on the bounty and charity of negroes for sustenance was going singlehanded into remote negro churches and interrupting the service to enter the pulpit and in his harsh, dead voice and at times with violent obscenity, preach to them humility before all skins

---

[14] For more on Joe as a scapegoat, see Baker 92-3.

lighter than theirs, preaching the superiority of the white race, himself his own exhibit A, in fanatic and unconscious paradox." (343-4).

Hines does not have an intellectual or theological basis for his white supremacy. Rather, it is based on hate. He is "violent," "fanatic," and "harsh." Further, his violent abilities seem to be more than just verbal. He is "one quarter conviction and three quarters physical hardihood" (343). Clearly, Hines both hates members of other races and has the "physical hardihood" to put his beliefs into action.

Similarly, Joe shows his racial hatred when he enters the pulpit. After killing Joanna, Joe interrupts a service at a local church: "And he begun to curse, hollering it out, at the folks, and he cursed God louder than the women screeching" (323). Unlike Hine's, Joe's sermon is coupled with not just the threat of violence, but with actual violence. Joe hits one of the congregants, and another pulls out a straight razor. Joe gets away before anyone is seriously injured, but this does not stop the congregation from sending someone to get the police. On one hand, Joe has become exactly like his grandfather. He sees religious ideology as justifying racial hatred. On the other hand, Joe has also become exactly what he hates. He is racially ambiguous, unsure whether he has the close connection with God he believes is a trait of the white race.

Importantly, Hines's indoctrination of Joe is not private; not only is preaching a public act, but Hines brings other people in on the violence in other very public ways, insuring that his ideology of hatred is not only passed on, but is also targeted at Joe. This begins at the orphanage where Joe is left. Hines, not identifying himself as Joe's grandfather, takes a job as the janitor so he can keep an eye on Joe. He watches the children playing outside, and he notes they have begun to call him by racial slurs. He insists he did not instigate this: "I never told them to say it, to call him in his rightful nature, by the name of his damnation. I never told them" (128). Despite this, he confirms to the dietician that this is true, though he will not make it public by going to the madam: the dietician says, "All I have to do is to think of some way to make the madam believe it. He wont tell her, back me up" (129). Hines advises her to "Wait. Like I waited. Five years I waited for the Lord to move and show His will. And He done it. You wait to" (128). At this phase, Hines is willing to passive-aggressively wait for Joe's violent destruction, a destruction which he will ultimately help to bring to fruition.

In a scene paralleling the children on the playground, Hines stirs up another crowd late in Joe's life. When Joe is taken to jail, Hines tries to stir up a lynch mob: "He said that he had a right to kill the nigger. He never said why, and he was too worked up and crazy to make sense even when somebody would stop him long enough to ask a question" (351). Hines has waited for what he believes is his moment and now will openly vie for the destruction of the impure blood he has hated ever since Joe was conceived. Hines's attempts to raise a mob prove unsuccessful, though it is a kind of lynch mob that ultimately kills Joe. Thus, Hines is responsible for Joe's ideology on several levels. He implants racial ambiguity on Joe, and then he teaches Joe to hate anyone not of pure white blood. Further, he puts this ideology in religious terms. As Michael Lackey suggests, "The God-concept has been consistently used to establish this closed epsitemologicl/ontological recursive loop and thereby marginalize and dehumanize culturally designated inferiors" (70).

Looking at Hines's influence on Joe's ideology is inherently problematic, however. Hines is an early influence on Joe, only influencing him in ways Joe never sees. Never do we see Hines actually teaching Joe anything; in fact, it is quite possible he never did. Further, there is little, if any, evidence Hines's theology is based on New England

Puritanism, though the people of Mottstown say, "They [the Hineses] are crazy; crazy on the subject of negroes. Maybe they are Yankees" (341). As such, Hines is not a particularly good example of the Northern ideology that I argue influences Joe.[15] Despite this, by presenting these scenes only in flashback and by providing no concrete Southern labels through which to understand Hines, the structure of the novel invites a comparison of Hines with both McEachern and Joanna. In addition to this, Joanna is given the only concrete (and decidedly Northern) label to explain these parallels. Before discussing how this understanding of the South through Northern labels enlightens the novel's themes, it is necessary to explore the more concrete forms of domination brought on by this ideology. Particularly, Hines's ideology does make Joe a subject whose identity cannot be understood in terms of legitimacy. As Michael Cobb says, "The question of race [Joe's] figure asks, communicated through a blasphemous, religious rhetoric, is actually a fundamental question about the inability to render, precisely, a story about 'real,' corporeal events—biological bodies with histories that must conventionally be told using two racially distinct historical values" (145). Thus, Joe's racial ambiguity makes his identity unreadable; he is subaltern in the way in which he cannot be understood by the dominant ideology, an ideology which created his ambiguity in the first place.[16] Hines's curse on Joe, in simplest terms, is Joe's lack of identity in a world where identity is linked to legitimacy of birth.

Joe's first interaction with a systematized ideology is from his adoptive father, Simon McEachern, a man who is importantly similar to Hines. McEachern is a sternly religious

---

[15] Importantly, Hines's ideology is not necessarily Southern either. Rather, Faulkner is silent on Hines's background. He could have New England roots; he could have spent every day of his life in Mississippi. As such, I rely on the parallels between his ideology and the more decidedly Northern ideologies of other characters rather than on his background to tie his character to my argument.

[16] Britton argues such unreadability is actually an advantage for a subaltern subject: "Opacity, then, transforms the status of the colonized subject's visibility from a source of vulnerability [...] to the active production of a visible but *unreadable* image" (24).

man, and actively indoctrinates Joe. Unlike Hines, McEachern's influence is not behind the scenes, not by calling Joe names and waiting for the right moment for his destruction. Rather, he teaches Joe doctrine by teaching him the catechism and taking him to church. Thus, I am now talking about institutions and ideology, not just some fanatic rantings. While this true, no denomination is ever identified; McEachern is just a fundamentalist. The only tie to any particular church is the catechism, which, while unnamed, would be considered foreign by many of the fundamentalist groups of the South whose focus is solely on the independence of each congregation to interpret scripture.

Importantly, McEachern never seems to consider that Joe has black blood. Clearly, he knows Joe is illegitimate, having adopted him with no clear record of his parentage. However, he does not seem to suspect that Joe could have black blood. McEachern is interesting, then, in the way he focuses the argument. Legitimacy is not an issue of race, or rather, only of race. Neither is it an offshoot of fanatical Southern racism. Rather, it is an ideological concern plaguing whites as well as blacks. In fact, Glissant would argue that it is an issue affecting whites more than blacks, for with legitimacy comes patrilineal responsibility for slavery: "So it is only to White people that the question—the nagging question of original responsibility—is addressed" (58).

Whereas, up until this point, the question of legitimacy has been tied to race, McEachern's concerns about legitimacy are tied to sex.[17] McEachern takes Joe into town one day, taking him to a restaurant that doubles as a whorehouse (or more properly, a whorehouse that doubles as a restaurant). McEachern tells Joe: "I'll have you remember that place. There are places in this world where a man may go but a boy, a youth of your age,

---

[17] I have elsewhere written on the way in which religion is the means through which McEachern (and other characters) project their own perceived flaws onto Joe. See *"Religion as an Agent of Projection in* Light in August*." Philological Review 33.2 (2007): 51-66.*

may not" (175). Joe later returns to the restaurant to meet up with Bobbie, one of the prostitutes, with whom he later has a relationship. When McEachern follows Joe and Bobbie to a country dance, McEachern confronts her. He calls her "Jezebel" and "harlot" (204). Importantly, McEachern does not know anything about Bobbie but her status in society: "Neither had McEachern ever seen the woman but once, and very likely then he had not looked at her, just as he had refused to listen when men spoke of fornication" (204). Joe and Bobbie's relationship is not one of a prostitute and a john. In fact, Joe does not even understand what Bobbie does for a living, at least not at first. McEachern does not know this; he has possibly never even looked at Bobbie, condemning her just because of her status in society. Given that Joe's status as a bastard is not much higher, Joe is presented with a paradox. He is taught to hate the illegitimate, but he himself is illegitimate.

McEachern's views are not unique to him; rather they are a part of an intricate theological system. This is clearly seen in the way in which McEachern juxtaposes sexualized violence with systematized theological learning. When Joe refuses to learn his catechism, McEachern takes him to the barn and whips him: "the boy stood, his trousers collapsed about his feet, his legs revealed beneath his brief shirt. He stood, slight and erect. When the strap fell he did not flinch, no quiver passed over his face" (149). McEachern insists that Joe continue to stand like this for another hour, in which he is to study his catechism. This cycle continues until Joe can hardly stand due to fatigue and lack of nutrition. Bush cites this scene when she rightly argues that McEachern teaches Joe "to associate manliness with sexualized violence" (485).

While Joe never memorizes his catechism, he does learn to express such sexualized violence towards the illegitimate, a fact clearly seen in Joe's first sexual experience. Joe and his friends bring a young black woman to a barn to take turns having sex with her. When it

becomes his turn, Joe lashes out with violence instead of coming on to her:

> But he could not move at once, standing there, smelling the woman smelling
> the negro all at once; enclosed by the womanshenegro and the haste, driven,
> having to wait until she spoke: a guiding sound that was no particular word
> and completely unaware. Then it seemed to him that he could see her—
> something, prone, abject [...] He was moving, because his foot touched her.
> Then it touched her again because he kicked her. He kicked her hard, kicking
> into and through a choked wail of surprise. (156-7).

Like McEachern in his rage against Bobbie, Joe's anger is directed not at a woman, but at a

concept. He is surrounded by "womanshenegro," a word which Valérie Loichot suggests

belongs to a Faulknerian category of words which are "all condensed compound words

whose signified is bigger than their signifiers." In this case, the concepts represented in the

word are classes of the disenfranchised and (at least according to McEachern's theology) the

illegitimate: women and blacks. This illegitimacy causes Joe to lash out, not the girl on the

barn floor.

This sexualized violence comes to a head in Joe's relationship with Joanna Burden.

He and Joanna have a violent sexual relationship, regularly enacting rape fantasies. This

pretend violence ultimately erupts into actual violence. Joanna attempts to shoot Joe, but the

gun misfires. Then, Joe cuts Joanna's throat with a straight razor. Even though Joanna is the

aggressor in the attack, Joe is arrested, and the town is shocked at the violent sexual

relationship. Joe's crime is not expiated in the town's mind until Joe is violently castrated in

his death, so that, in the words of his killer, he'll "let white women alone, even in hell" (464).

A detailed discussion of these two deaths is premature, however. Joanna is the

strongest figure of Northern ideology in the novel, and she has a profound effect on Joe, an

effect which transforms the ideologies of Hines and McEachern into an identity crisis for Joe.

While the ideologies of Hines and McEachern are described in the novel, Faulkner avoides

naming them. Instead, Joe plays out the domination he learns in his relationship with Joanna,

thus giving all of his understanding about ideology the vocabulary of Northern domination,

particularly conflating fundamentalism with Puritanism. As mentioned above, Joanna is the

daughter of a carpetbagger still considered a foreigner by most of the town. Joanna herself

describes her and her family's status: "And we were foreigners, strangers, that thought

differently from the people whose country we had come into without being asked or wanted"

(255). She represents Northern ideology. As Reed says, "Joanna's carpetbagger and

reformer instincts, far from evil in themselves, become evil when they rather than her human

feelings determine her relationship to Joe. They interpose external forms […] as a substitute

for human flexibility" (70). In other words, while the ideology may not be problematic, an

insistence on defining oneself by it is. This is what Joanna does. She insists that Joe define

himself by her ideology.

Joanna is notably a New England Puritan. As André Bleikasten points out, "Joanna's

father and grandfather represent a religion as extreme as Hines" or McEachern (85). Calvin

Burden, the grandfather, is himself the son of a minister. At a young age, Calvin leaves

home and marries a French woman. When he becomes a father, he returns to his Puritanism:

"He said then that he had denied the Catholic church a year ago for the sake of his son's soul;

almost as soon as the boy was born, he set about to imbue the child with the religion of his

New England forbears" (242). While Calvin is notably an abolitionist (a largely Northern

ideology), he also has concerns about legitimacy. He looks at himself and his own son and

sees "people of two different races" (242). Further, when his son Nathaniel goes to the West,

Calvin says, "if he lets them yellowbellied priests bamboozle him, I'll shoot him myself quick as I would a Reb" (244). Finally, when Nathaniel comes home having married an Hispanic woman, Calvin says, "Another damn black Burden" (247). Calvin's ideology does not consider any alteration in bloodline legitimate, even if the alteration is only to other European blood.

Nathaniel is little better when it comes to racial relations. He does not react violently and want to rid the world of people that are not pure blooded. Rather, he wants to help the illegitimate raise their social class. Regardless of his better intentions, he still views those of impure blood as illegitimate. He teaches Joanna:

> You must struggle, rise. But in order to rise, you must raise the shadow with you. But you can never lift it to your level. I see that now, which I did not see until I came down here. But escape it you cannot. The curse of the black race is God's curse. But the curse of the white race is the black man who will be forever God's chosen own because He once cursed him. (253)

Such condescension is little better than Calvin's hatred. While Nathaniel ostensibly wants to improve the condition of the illegitimate (since "black" for the Burden family really means "not-White"), he still believes their plight is due to some inherited condition of blood.

Joanna shares the condescension of her father. She ostensibly does good for many black causes throughout the South. During the day, she works at her desk; Joe learns that "what she received were business and private documents with fifty different postmarks and that what she sent were replies—advice, business, financial and religious, to the presidents and faculties and trustees, and advice personal and practical to young girl students and even alumnae of a dozen negro schools and colleges through the south" (233). Shortly before her death, Joanna tries to supply some of this charity to Joe. She asks Joe, "Do you realise [...] that you are wasting your life?" (268). She then offers to get him into law school, and then later a job with one of her charities: "she was trying to change his [life] too and make him something between a hermit and a missionary to negroes" (271). Importantly, she is not trying to *improve* his life; she is trying to *change* it. She repeatedly says that others will help Joe "on [her] account" (276). While Joanna's intention may be good and while her efforts to improve the lives of others may from time to time have been effective, her ideology still traps Joe in a world in which he is illegitimate and in which legitimacy is central to identity.

Joanna's condescension extends into her sex life with Joe, which is characterized by role-playing that casts Joe's identity in terms of stereotypes. Most notably, the middle phase of their relationship is marked by the repeated enactment of a rape fantasy. Joanna begins sending Joe notes with instructions on how to fulfill her fantasies[18]: "Sometimes the notes would tell him not to come until a certain hour [...] Now and then she appointed trysts beneath certain shrubs about the grounds, where he would find her naked, or with her clothing half torn to ribbons upon her" (259). In these fantasies, she would often call out to him in her sexual throes, calling him "Negro! Negro! Negro!" (260). Through games such as these, Joanna clearly establishes Joe's role as illegitimate. No matter the help she may promise him during the day, at night he is still the rogue black man who wants to ravish her.

Joanna, like Hines and McEachern, not only teaches Joe he is illegitimate, but she also teaches him he should hate himself for being illegitimate. Specifically, Joanna tries to indoctrinate Joe into her religion. She insists Joe pray with her to ask forgiveness for their sin (which was to pretend he was a legitimate sexual partner): "'Kneel,' she said. 'You wont even need to speak to Him yourself. Just kneel. Just make the first move" (280). Not only does she want Joe to believe her relationship with him is a sin, but she also wants him to believe he is not capable of asking for forgiveness for this sin on his own. She must be his

---

[18] Cobb suggests these notes are visible symbols of the attempt to make Joe a readable symbol: "Joe, throughout the novel, is always captured by little pieces of paper, such as these notes, that want to make him into a legible racial quantity" (149).

confessor, his intercessor. When Joe repeatedly refuses, she finally tries to use physical force, in this case a loaded revolver. Presumably, her attempt at force could have been successful had her revolver not misfired. Instead, Joe gets the upper hand and slits her throat. This use of prayer and force as instruments of domination directly parallels to the earlier actions of Hines and McEachern. In fact, in the context of the flashback, Joanna's influence on Joe becomes the culmination of the influences of Hines and McEachern.

Up to this point, I have explored the way in which the dominant ideology, represented in this novel by religion, traps Joe into an untenable position. Joe is indoctrinated by Hines, McEachern, and Joanna to believe he is illegitimate. This is not because he is black, but because his parentage cannot be proven to be not only white, but also Protestant (Catholics and Huguenots are considered just as illegitimate). Further, Joe is taught to despise—and act violently against—the illegitimate. Thus, Joe is left with a legacy of self-hatred based on racism both Northern and Southern in root, but couched in terms of Northern ideology in the wake of Reconstruction.

Certainly, Faulkner's conflation of racism, fundamentalism, and Northern ideology is not intended to excuse the influence of Southern ideology by blaming all the biases of the South on Northern influences. Rather, Faulkner's emphasis on Northern terminology serves to break down the dichotomy between North and South. Racism is a flaw of both regions, even if slavery is not. More importantly to my reading, however, this technique directly juxtaposes the condition of Joe Christmas with that of the South. Joe has no memory of his past, thus he must define himself through the teaching of others. Similarly, Southerners, no longer the most dominant class and thus separated from their past self-identity, must define themselves in terms of the North.

Loichot suggests Joe's untenable position is one endemic of the postcolonial moment. Using the terms of Glissant, Loichot argues, "In microcosm, Christmas represents a composite culture longing to become atavistic" (101). Loichot further explains: "Atavism, for Glissant, defines cultures which imagine a Genesis, an origin anchored in a specific place and time. This single beginning uncoils to the present, through a unidirectional and single lineage whereby the father (generally) transmits his name and legitimacy to the son" (100-1). Colonialism, by blending cultures, creates composite cultures which cannot rely on this single genesis and linear view of History (the Hegelian view earlier employed by Quentin in *Absalom*). Such composite cultures long to be atavistic, long for the legitimacy found therein. As Glissant says, "What is Yoknapatawpha? A composite culture that suffers from wanting to become an atavistic one and suffers in not being able to achieve that goal" (115).

Such a framework is useful in understanding the way in which Joe's condition parallels that of the South. Loichot rightly argues "that as a result of this violent uprooting, the community, symbolized by Christmas, finds no anchor to a known beginning" (102). She continues, "As a logical sequel to his errant birth, Christmas, like the naked migrants, cannot settle on a land and carries a constant feeling of homelessness about him" (102). Indeed, Joe is adrift: "the thousand streets ran as one, with imperceptible corners and changes of scene, broken by intervals of begged and stolen rides, on trains and trucks, and on company wagons with he at twenty and twentyfive and thirty sitting on the seat with his still hard face" (224). Further, Joe is pressed in his wandering by ideology: "It seemed to him that he could see himself being hunted by white men at last into the black abyss which had been waiting, trying, for thirty years to drown him and into which now and at last he had actually entered" (331). His wanderings are, indeed, central to understanding his character, as well as to understanding the postcolonial South, the South also being separated from its roots and searching for a new identity.

Unlike Loichot, however, I do not believe Joe is wandering because he is a displaced black man. Loichot says, "If we interpret Christmas through Glissantian theory, we can read his oceanic state as the past of 'Africans who have lived through the experience of deportation to the Americas'" (110). Certainly, Joe shares many qualities with other outcasts. Importantly, however, Joe is outcast not because of his birth, but because of his absence of one, or rather, the absence of the facts surrounding it. To remove Joe from this context is to put him again into the black/white dichotomy that leads to his demise. He is neither black nor white; he is without race.[19] Similarly, the condition of white aristocrats is not based on race, but rather on absence. The North did not create racism in the South, nor did it create fundamentalism. Rather, the North created an absence in the connection between the South and these deeply held ideals. While this absence may be a good thing, there is no Southern identity to fill the void left behind.

Completing this parallel between Joe and the South, Joe is literally killed by an embodiment of the military presence of the United States. After killing Joanna, Joe is imprisoned. He says he will plead not guilty to avoid the death penalty, yet he escapes from custody (in what some have called a passive suicide), knowing that the mob will kill him when he is found. His executioner becomes Percy Grimm, a local National Guardsman who proudly represents the national (that is, Northern) ideology by taking every opportunity to wear his uniform. Chuck Jackson, in his in-depth study of the National Guard during

---

[19] Faulkner, both in the text and in later lectures, takes great pains to emphasize Joe has no idea what race he is. Faulkner says, "Now with Christmas, for instance, he didn't know what he was. He knew that he would never know what he was, and his only salvation in order to live with himself was to repudiate mankind, to live outside the human race. And he tried to do that but nobody would let him" (*FIU* 118).

Faulkner's time, suggests that "For Percy Grimm, any identity other than an American identity—a nationally militarized identity—is a wasted identity, one divorced from power" (205). Grimm's ideology matches up with the other major influences in Joe's life, a fact revealed in his belief that the National Guard is even necessary in helping to prosecute a crime.[20] Jackson suggests that for Grimm, "A narrative that involves the accusation of interracial murder and rape constitutes a national emergency" (197). As Grimm chases Joe, Grimm is led as if in "blind obedience to whatever Player moved him on the Board" (462). This Player may be the God of the Burdens' religion or it may be the inevitable consequences of the prevalence of that religion. Regardless, Grimm is an avatar of the very ideology which has permeated Joe's life.[21]

Joe's death, then, is the only remedy for his plight, for in his death he is finally able to escape his doomed search for identity. The description of his death is filled with images of release: "from out the slashed garments about his hips and loins the pent black blood seemed to rush like a released breath. It seemed to rush out of his pale body like the rush of sparks from a rising rocket; upon that black blast the man seemed to rise soaring" (465). Joe's blood has escaped from the cage of his body; it no longer has to struggle to be legitimate. This is not to say he has found legitimacy in his death. I believe arguing this scene reveals Joe was actually black all along would be a mistake. Certainly, after the town hears Joe

---

[20] James Leo Spenko suggests other ways in which Grimm compares to the previous influences on Joe: "If Percy Grimm reminds us of both the sadistic stranger and Simon McEachern, he also reminds us of other brutal, punishing figures out of Joe's past" (256). See *"The Death of Joe Christmas and the Power of Words." Twentieth Century Literature* 28.3 (1982): 252-68.

[21] Jackson discusses another way in which Northern ideology is emphasized in Joe's death. Faulkner shows the death of Joe through the words of Gavin Stevens, the Ivy League-educated District Attorney of Jefferson, who is describing it to an Ivy Leaguer friend of his. Jackson explains: "Staged as a one-sided conversation between two ivy league-educated white men, Steven's monologue represents how the Gothic infiltrates modern racial thought, so much so that even Faulkner's Harvard-educated, state-representative lawman speaks of mixed-race in terms of a mythic—on might say eugenic—battle between good and evil blood pools" (194).

might possibly be a black man, they immediately begin to assume he is. As such, what they see is the lynching of a black man. The issue is resolved in their minds; it should not be resolved in the readers'. Instead, the repeated images of escape seem more pressing. Joe escapes from the cage of his body, and thus from his fate of being imprisoned by illegitimacy.

Joe's struggle, as I see it, is one shared metaphorically with the South. He is a part of a composite culture longing to be an atavistic one. He is indoctrinated into this culture by several major characters, characters whom Faulkner emphasizes are a part of a foreign (Northern) ideology. In search of this atavistic genesis, Joe has no choice but to try to be legitimate. His efforts are doomed, however, by his very condition; he never has hope of being legitimate, just as the South has no hope of being able to undo its loss in the Civil War. Instead, he can only die. Though I have argued Joe should not be viewed as a black man, these same facts could be said to apply to Joe even if he were black, and certainly blacks in the South suffered from this same ideology. I want to emphasize, however, that this is not entirely a racial issue, but a larger ideological one. As such, it would be useful to also look briefly at the character of Gail Hightower.

Hightower is much more like Quentin Compson, at least socioeconomically. He is an undoubtedly white man from a Southern family who is obsessed with the past. Cleanth Brooks compares the two: "One remembers characters like Faulkner's Quentin Compson or Gail Hightower. Their addiction to the sheer pastness of the past did prove disastrous" (268). Whereas the images of the blazing Sutpen's Hundred and of old Henry Sutpen wasting away in his bed haunt Quentin, the visions of what could have happened to Hightower's grandfather during the Civil War haunt Hightower. Also, critics have been quick to point out that Hightower's, like Quentin's, sexuality is ambiguous. Quentin is sexually obsessed with his sister, whether it is over his failure to fulfill his patriarchal role, his secret incestuous desires, or his homosexual desires for Shreve whose only feasible outlet is through the vicarious projection of them onto his sister. Similarly, the town questions Hightower's sexuality, assuming there is something unnatural about him because he is clearly not satisfying his wife. While I will not spend much time talking about either character's sexuality, the parallel between the two characters is too strong not to mention. In these respects, Hightower is much more like Quentin than like Joe.

Despite his position in a completely different socioeconomic class, Hightower is imprisoned by the search for legitimacy just like Joe. Like Joe, Hightower finds himself without a real past. While his parents do not abandon him, they are absent figures in his childhood. Hightower "was an only child. When he was born his father was fifty years old, and his mother had been an invalid for almost twenty years" (467). As such, he is raised by his father, already an old man.[22] The father was a pacifist chaplain during the Civil War and taught himself to be a doctor after the war, yet Hightower remembers his father in terms of absence: "The father who had been a minister without a church and a soldier without an enemy, and who in defeat had combined the two and become a doctor, a surgeon" (474). In fact, Hightower hardly views his parents as real people at all. He thinks of himself as "That son [who] grew to manhood among phantoms, and side by side with a ghost. The phantoms were his father, his mother, and an old negro woman" (474). While Hightower's race is not in question, his legitimacy is. His forbears are phantoms, absent from his life. He does not

---

[22] David Toomey argues the absence of Hightower's mother is central to understanding his character. See *"The Human Heart in Conflict:* Light in August*'s Schizophrenic Narrator."* Studies in the Novel *23.4 (1991): 425-69.*

feel the straight line of heredity springing from one mutual genesis. Instead, he is searching

for that genesis.

His search is carried out mainly through his fantasies. This begins when he finds his

father's old coat in the attic: "The garment was almost unrecognisable with patches. Patches

of leather, mansewn and crude, patches of Confederate grey weathered leafbrown now, and

one that stopped his very heart: it was blue, dark blue; the blue of the United States" (469).

Hightower begins imagining scenarios in which his pacifist father might have actually killed

an enemy soldier: "the cloth itself had assumed the properties of those phantoms who

loomed heroic and tremendous against a background of thunder and smoke and torn flags

which now filled his waking and sleeping life" (469). Hightower replaces one set of

phantoms with another, but his new phantoms promise legitimacy. They tie him to fighting

for what he considers the noble Southern cause. He is not one of the defeated, or rather is

only incidentally one of the defeated. Instead, he is part of the heroic army which he

imagines. He is not a child of the composite Reconstruction culture, but of the atavistic

antebellum Southern culture (which, of course, may well never have existed).

Hightower's ideology is clearly connected with Joe's in that Hightower's is also

espoused through religion. Particularly, Hightower mixes his sermons with tales of his

grandfather in the Civil War. His grandfather was killed in Jefferson, causing Hightower to

want to be given that commission. In reality, his grandfather was shot by a housewife while

stealing a chicken, after destroying a supply depot. Despite this fact, Hightower is obsessed

with his fantasy: "It was as if he couldn't get religion and that galloping cavalry and his dead

grandfather shot from the galloping horse untangled from each other, even in the pulpit" (62).

Further, when he preached, the dogma he was supposed to preach [was] all full of galloping cavalry and defeat and glory [...] it in turn would get all mixed up with absolution and choirs

of martial seraphim" (62-3). In Hightower's religion, "absolution" is connected with

"glory." Legitimacy is connected with some clear tie to an heroic past.

This obsession prevents him from having a real connection with other people, a fact

evident in his relationship with his wife. The town of Jefferson seems to be well aware that

Hightower's wife is dissatisfied: "the neighbors would hear her weeping in the parsonage in

the afternoons or late at night, and the neighbors knowing that the husband would not know

what to do about it because he did not even know what was wrong" (62). Hightower clearly

wants to do good deeds; he helps the black population in Jefferson at great personal risk to

himself. Yet he is unable to help his wife, because he is so obsessed with his own struggle

for legitimacy. In this way, he is something like Joanna, whose life is full of charity but who

is unable to actually help Joe because of her ideology. Eventually, Hightower's wife

commits suicide, and Hightower loses his pulpit, remaining in Jefferson despite his

humiliation to wait for the day when his grandfather might come galloping down the road.

Joe is ultimately killed in Hightower's house, and this seems to cause a major change

in Hightower. On the evening after Joe's death, Hightower sits by the window, watching as

always for his grandfather. This time, he uses the waiting for self-reflection:

> "And I know that for fifty years I have not even been clay: I have been a
> single instant of darkness in which a horse galloped and a gun crashed" [...]
> The wheel, released, seems to rush on with a long sighing sound. He sits
> motionless in its aftermath, in his cooling sweat, while the sweat pours and
> pours. The wheel whirls on. It is going fast and smooth now, because it is
> freed now of burden, of vehicle, axle, all. (491)

The language of the passage indicates the same kind of release and freeing as what happened

when Joe is killed. Hightower, however, is left alive and able to face the future. Leigh Anne

Duck suggests, "Gail ultimately determines that his investment in the vicarious trauma has prevented him from fulfilling his responsibilities in the present" (95). Joe's death, then, can truly be seen as the death of a scapegoat, for through his death Hightower is released from his struggle. While Joe's only release is escape, Hightower has a chance to continue in the world. I would argue this also gives a hopeful vision of the South. If Joe's death can allow Hightower to escape the past and move forward, perhaps the death of the antebellum South can allow the modern South to do the same.

Thus the theme of legitimacy, which is tied to Glissant's theory of composite and atavistic culture, is not merely based on racism in the novel, but also on the corporate identity crisis of the South in the wake of the Civil War. It is no surprise, then, that the novel is framed by the character of Lena Grove, a pregnant woman in search of her baby's father. Lena seems as though she should be the character most concerned with legitimacy. She is, after all, searching to make the baby legitimate by finding the father. As Reed says, "Lena's past is continually present because she is pregnant" (64). Yet Lena does not seem to be concerned with ideology. She is not really worried that she will never catch the father; in fact, she seems to expect not to. On the other hand, she is tied closely to the earth and not to society. She is barefooted, her feet getting covered constantly with the dust of the road. Taylor suggests Lena is the most free from society of Faulknerian characters: "In Lena Faulkner introduced a woman who by some miracle had never been indoctrinated by the Puritan whites around her [...] Lena had no repressed guilt to project onto anyone else" (58). Somehow Lena manages to escape the imprisonment of Joe and Hightower, though her social position should suggest she is concerned with illegitimacy.

In addition to this, many critics have suggested Lena's baby acts as a second Joe, one free from the struggle of legitimacy. After all, Mrs. Hines refers to the baby as Joe, presumably as a part of a delusion in which her husband's radical actions had not robbed her of Joe. Further, the baby is illegitimate and immediately fated to a life on the road, just as Joe is. Unlike Joe, however, this child will have the influence of Lena Grove rather than the ideology of Hines, McEachern, and Joanna. Patrick O'Donnel suggests, "the future configured in *Light in August* is but the past writ small, as if Christmas's voracious appetites had somehow been revivified and transmitted to the infant, who is all appetite, all desire focused and materially embodied" (116). Loichot agrees: "At the end of *Light in August*, however, we witness the beginning of a new form of plural composite histories surviving the atavistic patriarchic history burned in the conflagration of the big house" (111). Lena and her baby, then, represent an alternative to the end to which Joe comes and envision a possible future South that has resolved its identity crisis.

Lena is somehow tied to an atavistic culture, to the earth itself, to a genesis transcending the dominant ideology—ideology of any sort, in fact. *Light in August* does not explain why this is, however; nor does it offer a possible course of action to other characters. Rather, Joe is forced to escape life, becoming a scapegoat that might allow Hightower to salvage his life. Certainly the scapegoat has a role within postcolonial literature, and many postcolonial authors have found this small act of resistance to be as far as some subaltern people can go to have a voice. Faulkner seems to suggest there is a way to go further, however, a way for the South to join Lena, even if only imperfectly. In *Light in August*, he presents this hope in the form of the baby. In *Absalom, Absalom!*, he presents hope in the narrative structure itself, for though Quentin never develops a "creole poetics," Faulkner seems to. In *Go Down, Moses*, however, Faulkner actually compares atavistic and composite cultures side by side, presenting a character stuck in between. This character, Ike McCaslin, has a choice of which culture to belong to, though an imperfect one. His character, then, is the obvious next step in my argument.

IV. Genesis and Digenesis in *Go Down, Moses*

Go Down, Moses represents a significant shift of focus in my argument.[23] The stories within this collection do deal with some of the issues discussed above, of course. The central character, Isaac "Uncle Ike" McCaslin, is concerned with the past and with legitimacy, like Quentin or Joe. Carl E. Rollyson, Jr., suggests, "What all these episodes have in common is Ike's obsession with the past and his constant attempt to atone for its evil" (106). Further, Taylor notes how Ike's search for identity is hindered by Northern ideology: "Issac had no sympathy with the northern role in Reconstruction; that had been a 'dark corrupt and bloody time.' Carpetbaggers were a 'race even more alien to the people whom they resembled in pigment...than to the people whom they did not" (125). However, unlike the previously mentioned characters, Ike abandons the ideology that would imprison him, opting instead for what he believes is the Native American formula, repudiating his inheritance and denouncing ownership of the land. Taylor notes how different this approach is from the other characters: "White aristocrats locked into their inherited outlook [like Quentin], had trouble understanding the curse; when they looked for an alternative to paternalism, all they could see was the Manichaean Puritanism that had produced the abolitionist crusade [like Joe's relationship with Joanna].[24] But Isaac had been able to burrow under that" (127). The way in which Ike "burrows" under the dominant ideology is based on his understanding of Native American culture, an understanding which can be more fully understood when read in light of Glissant's discussion of composite cultures and digenesis.

---

[23] For a more detailed discussion of many of the parallels between *Go Down, Moses* and other literature of the Americas, see *Hosam Aboul-Ela. "The Political Economy of Southern Race:* Go Down, Moses, *Spatial Inequality and the Color Line." Mississippi Quarterly: The Journal of Southern Culture 57 (2003): 55-64.*

[24] Taylor suggests religion in *Go Down, Moses* is used significantly differently than religion in novels such as *Light in August*. Particularly, Taylor suggests Faulkner draws an intentional parallel between God and a plantation owner in *Go Down, Moses*. While this is hardly a flattering picture, it is at least distinctly Southern and stands in contrast to Northern Puritanism (127-8).

Native Americans appear in various places in Faulkner's writing, particularly in some of his early short stories.[25] Consistent with his strategies of dealing with black culture, Faulkner rarely tries to enter into the minds of his Native American characters. Instead, he portrays the culture from the outside, in a way that some have argued is patronizing, especially in the early stories. Faulkner seems to have a very specific purpose in using the culture, however; the Native Americans in Yoknapatawpha serve as a bridge between the white aristocracy and the freed blacks. As Louis M. Dabney says, "Dispossessed by a more 'advanced' civilization, [the Native Americans] shared this with both the white South and the black, and had mingled their blood with both" (18). Native American culture, then, is a neutral narrative space in which Faulkner can explore the issues of the South in the absence of the stark dichotomy often caused by race.

Further, Native Americans in Yoknapatawpha are unique to other groups in that they are still connected with their native land. They have not been taken from their homes and forced to live and work in the New World. Neither have they set out to form an empire, slowly losing their own culture to a composite culture. Faulkner emphasizes this connection, tying characters such as Sam Fathers directly to the land. Fathers seems to have no father but the land; he is completely apart from society and the struggle for legitimacy. This connection is what attracts Ike to Fathers and to his culture. More importantly to the present argument, this connection is what attracts a closer postcolonial reading. Native Americans have the connection to an atavistic culture that Faulkner's white aristocrats have sought.

---

[25] For a more complete discussion of all of Faulkner's writings about Native Americans, see *Louis M. Dabney. The Indians of Yoknapatawpha: A Study in Literature and History. Baton Rouge: Louisiana State UP, 1974.* For a more specific discussion of postcolonial themes in the early short stories see *Annette Trefzer. "Postcolonial Displacements in Faulkner's Indian Stories of the 1930s." Faulkner in the Twenty-First Century: Faulkner and Yoknapatawpha, 2000. Ed. Robert Hamblin and Ann J. Abadie. Jackson, MS: UP of Mississippi, 2003. 68-88.*

For Glissant, composite cultures are not linearly connected to a genesis. He says, "Every composite culture originates from a digenesis (which is not, in every case, a catastrophe such as slavery) whose component parts are multiplied ad infinitum" (195). This digenesis has more impact on a postcolonial subject than the dominant stories about a genesis (which the subject no longer feels connected to). Glissant notes how many postcolonial cultures resist the dominant ideology by questioning genesis narratives: "The Creole stories of the Antilles, for example, question the Creation myth or throw it into turmoil" (194). Glissant does recognize degrees of this, however. He does not suggest Faulkner's purpose is to undermine the Christian creation story, although characters such as Ike seem to read the story in a very different way from characters such as Cass, a fact made clear in the commissary scene. Glissant argues, "Even if we believe that the tales and stories Faulkner heard in his youth never challenged the foundational authority of a Genesis, the way Creole tales do, we can at least believe that he sensed in these tales a denial of a challenge to the absolute legitimacy of a dynastic bloodline" (197). For Ike, the challenge to this bloodline, and thus the hope for a return to an atavistic culture that can actually satisfy him, is personified in the character of Sam Fathers.

Jay S. Winston suggests, "This sense of, or need for, ancestry is manifest in the naming of Faulkner's most prominent Indian, the mixed-blood Sam Fathers" (130). Fathers's last name (which is actually short for Had-Two-Fathers) is an indication of his unusual heritage. Fathers is the son of Ikkemotubbe-Doom, a local chief. Doom does not acknowledge Fathers, however, Fathers being raised by his mother and step-father, who are both black. Dabney explains, "In becoming Doom's son, Sam acquires a father who will not acknowledge him, as Old Carothers and Sutpen will not acknowledge their black sons"

(124). Fathers, like Joe and perhaps Bon, is of mixed blood, but for Fathers the main mixture is black and Native American, although he does have a small amount of white blood. Dabney argues that this combination of blood is the key to Fathers's freedom from the search for legitimacy: "How, though, can [Faulkner] reconcile the redeeming virtues of the hunt with the Indians' collaboration in their own downfall? [...] Sam Fathers' mixed blood is the answer. He is an Indian whose background of slavery exempts him from the guilt of the owners" (143). Since Fathers's two fathers free him from the search of legitimacy, he at times seems to be free of any parentage whatsoever, instead finding his identity with the land.

Fathers's connection with the land is central. Faulkner seems to suggest this is based on some sort of arcane knowledge; according to Ike, "When [Fathers] was born, all his blood on both sides, except the little white part, knew things that had been tamed out of our blood so long ago that we have not only forgotten them, we have to live together in herds to protect ourselves from our own sources" (161). Ike believes Fathers's blood should have made him "his own battleground," but there is no outward sign of Fathers's struggle. Instead, he seems to be separate from society. Sam does not seem constrained by traditional racial boundaries. Even though Ike believes his black blood should determine that he behave as a black man, he did "White man's work, when [he] did work" (163). Most of the time, though, he sat around the general store talking, as if he had the same amount of leisure time as a landowner. For Fathers, his arcane connection with the earth is his progenitor.

Fathers passes on this connection to Ike through the annual hunting trip. When Ike kills his first deer in "The Old People," Fathers anoints the boy with the animal's blood: "They were the white boy, marked forever, and the old dark man sired on both sides by savage kings" (159). This ritual is more than just symbolic. Fathers is responsible for Ike's training in how to successfully kill an animal in a hunt. Further, Fathers teaches Ike his arcane knowledge of the land is more important than his actual heritage, or is at least a part of his actual heritage. Fathers takes Ike to find the buck the hunting party is searching for, but when he finds it, Sam keeps Ike from killing it. Instead, he greets the buck in what is presumably his ancestral language, saying "Oleh, Chief [...] Grandfather" (177). This greeting not only connects nature, in the form of the buck, to patrilineal ancestry—the buck becomes Ike's progenitor, and not Old Carothers—but it also establishes this connection as something atavistic by using the language of Fathers's Native American ancestors.

This connection becomes more pronounced in "The Bear," where Fathers is connected to the elusive prey, the bear Old Ben. Faulkner portrays Old Ben as the patriarch of the bear world: "he's the head bear. He's the man" (190). Old Ben has earned his legacy: he has "earned a name such as a human man could have worn and not been sorry" (221). Old Ben, like the buck, is part of a legendary group of progenitors. Importantly, Fathers is part of this group as well: "only Sam and Old Ben and the mongrel Lion were taintless and incorruptible" (183). Fathers has become the progenitor he taught Ike to respect. He is the inheritor of the arcane knowledge, the legacy not built on the legitimacy of blood.

This transformation of Fathers from Ike's mentor to Ike's progenitor is played out through the hunt for Old Ben. Fathers councils Ike to approach the bear without a weapon if he wants to see him. Ike does. This does not stop the bear from being killed later that season, however, an event which puts Fathers on his deathbed: "the wild man not even one generation from the woods, childless, kinless, people-less—motionless, his eyes open but no longer looking at any of them" (236). The doctor diagnoses Fathers with shock, saying the condition is not fatal. Despite this, Fathers dies, perhaps with the help of Boon Hogganbeck.

Fathers's passing is timed with that of Old Ben and of Lion, Fathers's hunting dog that is a

patriarch to dogs in much the way Old Ben is a patriarch to bears. Further, Fathers's passing

coincides with the recession of the wilderness. As such, his death (and thus his character) is

inextricably tied to arcane knowledge about the wilderness.

Sensing that such arcane knowledge, such a connection to an atavistic genesis, can

free him from the guilt of his inheritance, Ike tries to develop a connection with the land akin

to what Fathers had. After all, Ike spends much time with his mentor and has a natural talent

as an outdoorsman; as General Compson says to Ike's cousin Cass:

> You've got one foot straddled into a farm and the other foot straddled into a
> bank; you aint even got a good hand-hold where this boy [Ike] was already an
> old man long before you damned Sartorises and Edmondses invented farms
> and banks to keep yourselves from having to find out what this boy was born
> knowing and fearing too maybe but without being afraid, that could go ten
> miles on a compass because he wanted to look at a bear none of us had ever
> got near enough to put a bullet in and looked at the bear and came the ten
> miles back on the compass in the dark; maybe that's the why and the
> wherefore of farms and banks. (240)

Not surprisingly, Compson's comment comes immediately before Fathers's death. The

arcane knowledge Ike was "born knowing" is now his defining attribute. He is no longer a

boy learning from the old Native American man. He is now the same sort of man as Fathers

was. And Compson recognizes this as a latent quality of Ike, not as the logical end to a

natural progression.

Ike's connection with Fathers is clearly seen in the tales concerning Ike's childhood.

This begins in "The Old People," which describes Fathers's teaching Ike to hunt. David W.

Robinson suggests this story "comments ironically on the idyllic view of nature and hunting

that Sam passes on to Ike" (199). Much of Ike's training involves his and Fathers's standing still and waiting for deer to pass by: "Each morning Sam would take the boy out to the stand allotted him. [...] But they would stand there, Fathers a little behind him and without a gun himself" (169). The image of the two standing side by side in the woods, perfectly still, for long periods of time emphasizes their sameness. At this point, however, the comparison is not complete. Fathers is standing a little behind; he is still the teacher, not the peer. Further, Fathers is without a gun.

By "The Bear," Ike has also learned to leave his gun behind. He realizes from Fathers's teaching that if he wants to see Old Ben, he will have to approach him unarmed: "He was hunting right, upwind, as Sam had taught him, but that didn't matter now. He had left the gun; by his own will and relinquishment he had accepted not a gambit, not a choice, but a condition in which not only the bear's heretofore inviolable anonymity but all the ancient rules and balances of hunter and hunted had been abrogated" (198). Because Faulkner frames this in epic terms, Ike's acceptance becomes the audience's acceptance; Richard Poirier argues, "Faulkner's style makes the reader's experience analogous to the hero's. The style requires that the reader divest himself of most of the conventional assumptions about hunting, people, and things that he brings to the story" (51). As such, the audience must accept that Ike's transformed view of the hunt is significant to his character.

Although Ike does become like Fathers in the wilderness, he is less successful at translating his atavistic knowledge back to the rest of his life. He rejects his inheritance (the digenesis of slavery) in favor of the land (the genesis of the native culture). Though he is the oldest white heir of Old Carothers (and the only white heir of the male line), he has legal right to the McCaslin plantation. He yields this right to his cousin Cass. When Cass balks at Ike's decision, Ike replies, "I cant repudiate it. It was never mine to repudiate" (245). Ike tries to be separate from patrilineal corruption in the way Fathers was. Taylor suggests, "That was why, instead of trying to save blacks from themselves by perpetuating the plantation, whites had to do something else" (129). For Ike, this something else is ending the plantation system by ending inheritance in general.

Ike continues to try to explain his repudiation to Cass. Ike's decision is based on his understanding of the Christian genesis, a genesis which he portrays in a rather unorthodox, though still linear, way. Ike says, God was "Not impotent: He didn't condone; not blind, because He watched it. And let me say it. Dispossessed of Eden. Dispossessed of Canaan, and those who dispossessed him dispossessed him dispossessed" (247). For Ike, dispossession is all part of God's plan, and Ike is a minor player in that plan: "Yes. If He could see Father and Uncle Buddy in Grandfather He must have seen me too.—an Isaac born into a later life than Abraham's and repudiating immolation" (270). Cass's view of the repudiation is quite different. Rollyson rightly notes that for Cass, "The active force in history is not God, but man, and man has established his own relationship to the land" (119). Cass's view corresponds more directly with the dominant view, his opinion accepting standard laws regarding land ownership, as well as patrilineal descent. Ike's opinion stands in sharp contrast to Cass's, Ike seeing dispossession as the driving force in God's plan.

Ike's argument with his cousin extends through the generations to his cousin's grandson, Roth. In "Delta Autumn," Ike is now an old man and Roth is in charge of the former McCaslin plantation. Ike has lived in virtual seclusion for decades, and Roth points out how little Ike's repudiation has helped. Ike, in the process of scolding Roth for taking a black mistress, says, "There are good men everywhere, at all times. Most men are. Some are just unlucky, because most men are a little better than their circumstances give them a chance to be. And I've known some that even the circumstances couldn't stop" (329). Roth replies, "So you've lived almost eighty years [...] And that's what you finally learned about the other animals you lived among. I suppose the question to ask you is, where have you been all the time you were dead?" (329). The central point of contention between the two is the nature of society. Roth argues the only reason people behave is the constraints put on them and enforced by societal institutions. Ike, however, argues that people behave because they are good.

Most critics agree with Roth, acknowledging that Ike's repudiation is ineffectual. Warwick Wadlington suggests, "Faulkner's commentators have pointed out that Ike condemns himself to futility with his well-meaning decision to wall his desire off from such a flawed public, social world by giving away his inheritance" (211). Margaret M. Dunn sees Ike's futility in his inability to save the things he cares about: "In 'freeing' himself from the responsibilities of managing the McCaslin land holdings, Ike renders himself powerless to stop or at least appreciably retard the destruction of his beloved wilderness" (411). Further, Ike is unable to help characters like Mollie[26] Beauchamps (in "Go Down, Moses") in a way that might have been transformative. Finally, Rollyson finds that Ike neglects his responsibility to pass on his realization about the flawed nature of Southern society to anyone else: "By not becoming actively involved in his heritage, Ike not only deprived Roth of a chance to see Ike's principles in operation but left him to work out very complex problems

---

[26] It is worth noting that Mollie's name is sometimes spelled "Molly." Usually, "Molly" is used by black narrators (or more properly, in the dialogue of black characters, as Faulkner shies away from having black narrators), while "Mollie" is used in the dialogue of white characters and in the third person narration. I have chosen the latter for purely stylistic reasons. Faulkner generally uses conventional spellings in the third-person narration and unconventional spellings (when necessary) in the dialogue. As such, I assume that "Mollie" was supposed to be the convention. One might also argue that the question is one of authority, and Mollie's name is connected to her identity, which means that the dialectical spelling might be more authoritative. It is also possible that this was an intentional inconsistency across Faulkner's drafts.

for himself" (110).   After all, Ike claims to be trying to make a better world for his son, but in the end, he does not succeed in having a son or passing on his knowledge in any way.

Further, some critics see Ike's repudiation as merely a mask for the same ideology he attempts to renounce. In "Delta Autumn," Ike stays behind while the rest of the group goes out to hunt. Roth tells him a woman (Roth's black mistress) will be stopping by and asks Ike to tell her "No" and to give her an envelope full of money. The exchange between Roth's mistress and Ike seems to reveal the same racism Ike is condemning in society. Ike suggests the woman move to the North: "You are young, handsome, almost white; you could find a black man who would see in you what it was you saw in him" (346). Further, after long avoiding such language, Ike says to her, "You're a nigger?" (344). The woman calmly reacts to this: "'Old man,' she said, 'have you lived so long and forgotten so much that you dont remember anything you ever knew or felt or even heard about love?" (346). Her accusation is the same as Roth's: Ike has repudiated his inheritance and thus has lost any ability he might have had to make a difference in society.

Baker disagrees with these critics, however. He says, "Only the harshest critic would condemn Ike for failing to end racism in his lifetime. He might have done more, but he could never have done enough" (120). Further, Baker gives Ike credit for having recognized the position his inheritance puts him in: "Ike boldly recognizes the curse under which his land suffers but cannot imagine a way out of it" (120). Baker summarizes, "Such is probably the most comprehensive assessment of Issac McCaslin, a decent man who chooses not to do evil but fails to do good" (120). In light of Ike's cultural context, Baker sees this as admirable. Ike is the type of good man who is just a little better than his circumstances, the type of good man Ike himself describes in "Delta Autumn."

My purpose is not to morally account for Ike's actions, however. It matters not for the current argument whether Ike was correct in his decision to renounce his heritage. What is important is that Ike never seems to escape the dominant culture as he intends to do, forming instead an alternative linear narrative that is no more effectual than the dominant linear narrative. He recognizes the deep flaws in his own culture, and he tries to walk away from them. In the end, however, he shows the same prejudices and mindsets as the other characters in the stories. Dunn says Faulkner "finds, in sum, that freedom is an illusion" (423). For all Ike's lecturing, he is no different from his cousins. As Taylor argues, "Isaac's beliefs about miscegenation had never been any different from Cass's and Roth's. All mulattos, he seemed to be saying, were tragic" (153). Importantly, Ike may represent a necessary first step, recognition. But he is never able to realize the change of mindset he recognizes as necessary. Ike wants a connection to an atavistic genesis, like he saw in Fathers and like Faulkner earlier portrayed in Lena, but since he cannot have this connection, his story is tragic.

V. Conclusion: *Go Down, Moses* and Faulkner's Alternative Poetics

Ike's story builds upon the themes explored above, and as such would seemingly serve as a nice conclusion to my argument. However, to stop after the story of Ike would be to come no further than I already did with *Light in August*. With Ike, the need for an atavistic genesis is more explicit, and the character of Fathers is more deeply explored than was the character of Lena. Nevertheless, Ike is in many ways a very similar character to Quentin or Joe. Further, to stop after the story of Ike would be to ignore the format of *Go Down, Moses,* which is a collection of short stories and not a novel.[27] While much of the subject matter of the stories expands the character of Ike, many moments—and even the entire story "Pantaloon in Black"—seem tangential to Ike's story. Understanding how these stories fit in with the narrative of Ike may help clarify Faulkner's purpose for the collection.

Specifically, I am drawn back to Ladd's focus on "creole poetics" in *Absalom*. This is appropriate in light of Ike's inability to escape a linear narration, and indeed the alternative voices in *Moses* are distinctly nonlinear. *Moses* goes further, however. Whereas *Absalom* belies Quentin's reliance on a linear view of History by employing a distinctly nonlinear narrative, *Moses* presents a nonlinear narrative that is full of a variety of alternative voices. Such alternative voices have long been problematic in postcolonial criticism. Edward W. Said notes the difficulty in portraying a different culture: "One ought again to remember that all cultures impose corrections upon raw reality, changing it from free-floating objects into units of knowledge" (67). Said recognizes this alternation as a necessity: "It is perfectly natural for the human mind to resist the assault on it of untreated strangeness [...] To the Westerner, however, the Oriental was always *like* some aspect of the West" (67). Clearly,

---

[27] For an interesting exploration of the publication history of *Go Down, Moses*, see *Marvin Klotz. "Procrustean Revision in Faulkner's* Go Down, Moses." *American Literature 37.1 (1965): 1-16.*

Said's emphasis is on the relationship between the East and the West, specifically focusing on the way in which the West creates the "Orient" as Other. Despite this, Said's observations are relevant to Faulkner. In *Moses*, Faulkner uses the voices of other subaltern groups. The structure is disjointed, however, allowing the voices to stand alone. Faulkner does not try to make these alternative narratives *like* Ike's narratives, but leaves them standing in juxtaposition as nonlinear alternatives to the dominant narration.

The stories of *Go Down, Moses* represent an alternative sort of poetics, one that is more fluid, and sometimes more playful, than Ike's. Dunn suggests, "Faulkner thus shows that only those who have freed themselves from the burden of the past by accepting it, not by idealistically 'renouncing' it like Ike, can move unfettered into the future" (411). I would clarify the statement, saying instead that freedom comes not from acknowledging the past, but from not trying to encapsulate the past in a linear narrative, such being the lesson Quentin never learned in *Absalom, Absalom!*. *Go Down, Moses* shows that Faulkner at least has learned the lesson, applying an alternative poetics to his works.

Faulkner's alternative poetics is first seen in "Was," a story of the playful nature of the courtship of Ike's mother and father, which is juxtaposed with the games surrounding the courtship of Tomey's Turl (born Terrell Beauchamp, one of Old Carothers black descendents). Importantly, the first section of the story establishes the central narration of this story is intended to be contrasted with Ike's narration. The story opens: "Isaac McCaslin, 'Uncle Ike', past seventy and nearer eighty than he ever corroborated any more, a widower now and uncle to half a county and father to no one […] this was not something participated in or even seen by himself" (3). The picture of Ike is a stark one. He is old, and he has not succeeded in having a family. But he is not a character in "Was." He did not see the events, and perhaps never even heard about them. As such, these events are set apart thematically from the stories that focus on Ike.

The playfulness of the courtship rituals in "Was" is established through the escape of Tomey's Turl, the slave of Uncle Buck (Ike's father) and Uncle Buddy, the twin white sons of Old Carothers McCaslin. Buck and Buddy do not treat their slaves like slaves, however, living in a cabin on the property while their slaves live in the unfinished big house. Further, they allow their slaves a certain measure of freedom, purposefully not locking the back door of the house at night. Tomey's Turl takes advantage of this freedom to escape to the neighboring plantation to visit Tennie, a slave with whom he has had a longtime affair. He clearly does not see his escape as a big deal: "Tomey's Turl would go there to hang around Mr. Hubert's girl, Tennie, until somebody came and got him" (5). Buck and Buddy do not seem to care either, offering to sell Tomey's Turl to Hubert, or even give him to Hubert and pay his room and board. Hubert refuses the offer, though, so Buck must go after Tomey's Turl. This is not to punish the runaway though: "And if somebody didn't go and get Tomey's Turl right away, Mr Hubert would fetch him back himself, bringing Miss Sophonsiba, and they would stay for a week or longer" (6). Miss Sophonsiba is the unmarried sister of Hubert; as such, she is in search of a spouse and would take advantage of the visit to Buck and Buddy as an opportunity to court Buck.

What follows is a humorous chase scene, in which Buck follows Tomey's Turl and tries to catch him, Tomey's Turl always staying a few steps ahead of Buck. Since Tomey's Turl's intention is not to escape, but to see Tennie, Buck eventually catches up with him. Importantly, this exchange ends in a game: Buck and Hubert play a hand of poker to see who will buy the other's slave in order to stop the cycle of escape and reclamation. Hubert adds an extra term to the wager: "If I win, you take Sibbey without dowry" (27). The playfulness surrounding Tomey's Turl's escape has expanded to an actual game between Buck and Hubert, the outcome of which will determine Buck's marital status. Buck wins this game, Hubert refusing to call Buck's hand.

The games do not stop with poker, however. Sophonsiba is much more determined than Hubert, and catches Buck in his actions of the night before. When Uncle Buck is looking for his room, he is worried about accidentally going into Sophonsiba's room by mistake. He reasons, "Likely hers will be at the back [...] Where she can holler down to the kitchen without having to get up. Besides, an unmarried lady will sholy have her door locked with strangers in the house" (19). Buck reasons incorrectly, however, and lies down next to her by mistake. Not only does this mistake lead to Hubert's anger, but it also leads to his insistence that Buck marry her (and subsequently their wager regarding the dowry). Though Buck wins the poker game, he is unable to avoid Sophonsiba and marries her. This is no shotgun wedding, however; the game never stops. Buck marries Sophonisiba because she won, not because Hubert forces him to. Buck's last line of the story is significant: "Damn the fox [...] Go on and start breakfast. It seems to me I've been away from home a whole damn month" (29). While he is clearly exasperated, he is not angry. For Ike, marriage is an obsessive male compulsion about progeny; in contrast, Buck's and Sophonsiba's marriage is a game between a reluctant man and a woman.

"The Fire and the Hearth" also juxtaposes Ike's character with an alternative poetics. In this case, Lucas Beauchamp[28] (Tomey's Turl's son) serves as a direct parallel to Ike.

---

[28] Zender discusses the ways in which Homi Bhabha's concept of "hybridity" enlightens the understanding of Lucas's character. See *"Lucas Beauchamp's Choices." Faulkner in the Twenty-First Century: Faulkner and Yoknapatawpha, 2000. Ed. Robert Hamblin and Ann J. Abadie. Jackson, MS: UP of Mississippi, 2003. 119-36.*

Lucas and Ike are the only direct male descendents of Old Carothers. Whereas Ike repudiates

his inheritance, Lucas is never in a position to inherit the land at all, because he is an

illegitimate black heir. Lucas does embrace his heritage, however, sometimes to the point of

obsession. Unlike Ike, however, Lucas is able to move fluidly despite his obsession with

legitimacy. He is part of a fruitful marriage and has kids. In part because of his wife's

insistence, he is able to reject his obsession in favor of an alternative, a family.

Because of his obsession, Lucas twice confronts Ike's cousins. First, when Lucas is

young, his wife Mollie becomes Zack Edmonds's nursemaid after Zack's wife dies in

childbirth. Lucas begins to incorrectly suspect that Mollie is having an affair with Zack; he

thinks, "*He keeps her in the house with him six months and I don't do nothing: he sends her*

back to me and I kills him. It would be like I had done said aloud to the whole world that he

never sent her back because I told him to but he give her back to me because he was tired of

her" (48). Following that logic, Lucas heads to the house to confront Zack, bringing with

him a razor with which to kill him. He says to Zack, "You know I wasn't afraid, because you

knowed I was a McCaslin too and a man-made one. And you never thought that, because I

am a McCaslin too, I wouldn't. You never even thought that, because I am a nigger too, I

wouldn't dare. No. You thought that because I am a nigger I wouldn't even mind" (52).

Lucas's anger is based not so much on what Zack has supposedly done, but more on the way

Zack treats him as illegitimate. While this conflict is resolved without harm to either party,

Lucas is clearly established as a character who is obsessed with legitimacy.

Lucas's obsession does not wane with time. In a parallel scene with Lucas as an old

man, he goes to the house to tell Roth (Zack's son) that Lucas's daughter's fiancé has a

whiskey still on the land, hoping this lie will cause Roth to have the unwelcome fiancé arrested. He says to Roth, "I've lived on this place since I was born, since before your pa

was. And you or him or old Cass either aint never heard of me having truck with any kind of

whisky except that bottle of town whisky you and him give Molly Christmas" (59). Even

though Lucas is lying, it is important that he has still not let go of his vision of himself in

relationship to the Edmondses. Since he is the closest male descendent to Old Carothers, he

makes it clear he views himself as equal to (and perhaps better than) the Edmondses. As

Taylor says, "Lucas patterned himself after old Crothers. His pride in his heritage from this

ancestor amounted almost to a phobia" (138).

Lucas's obsession with legitimacy transforms into an obsession with money. Since

Lucas is unable to receive the inheritance he insists is rightfully his, he tries instead to get an

inheritance on his own. Despite Roth's wishes, he distills bootleg whiskey on the land. In

the process of burying his still one night, he finds a coin and assumes there must be buried

treasure. He takes a mule from Roth and offers it to a salesman in exchange for a metal

detector and spends all his nights looking for the buried treasure. He thinks, "*I probably aint*

even made a scratch yet on the kind of luck that can wait unto [sic] *I am sixty-seven years*

old, almost too old to even want it, to make me rich (60). Karl F. Zender suggests Lucas's

actions, as well as his speech in the previous examples, is his way of reclaiming the

inheritance which he has lost: these "can be understood not as interpellation but as

acquisition, as an aggressive and ambitious co-optation for his own purposes of the voice of

the dominant order" ("Lucas" 131). Such co-optation is the logical extension of Lucas's

obsession.

While Lucas is obsessed (like Ike, Quentin, or Hightower), his fluid relationships free

him from his obsession in the end. Dunn rightly argues, "Lucas' heritage is one of personal and class exploitation. Nevertheless, it is a heritage which manages through pride and dignity to live with and transcend, in contrast to Ike McCaslin who fails to free himself from a heritage which he publicly repudiates" (414). Lucas's escape from his obsession comes largely through the agency of his wife. Mollie begins insisting on a divorce because of the obsession. She changes her mind only after Lucas backs down. Lucas's last words of the story are humorous, similar in tone to Buck's last line of "Was." He says, "I don't give no man advice about his wife" (75). This shift in tone is very important. Lucas has been as obsessed with legitimacy as any of the white characters, yet the voice of his wife cracks through his obsession and changes his tone, as well.

The voices of the alternate narrators stand in contrast not only to the story of Ike but also to the dominant white voice throughout the novel. This is made particularly clear in the middle story, "Pantaloon in Black." This story has none of the playfulness of the previous stories. In fact, it is quite stark, relating Rider's grief over the death of his wife and his subsequent murder of a white man. Faulkner first tells Rider's story, then has a white man, who misses the central conflict of Rider's grief, re-tell the story.[29]

"Pantaloon in Black" begins with Rider's grief told in the third-person: "He stood in the worn, faded clean overalls which Mannie herself had washed only a week ago, and heard the first clod strike the pine box. Soon he had one of the shovels himself" (131). After the funeral, Rider begins acting uncharacteristically. He begins drinking and ignoring his close family members. Further, he sees Mannie's ghost: "He stopped at once, not breathing again, motionless, willing his eyes to see that she had stopped too" (136). In order to avoid the ghost (and thus the grief) Rider refuses to stay at home, going instead to a craps game at the

---

[29] Taylor suggests Faulkner creates a version of Ike's vision of blacks but undermines it, both questioning Ike and refusing to try to step into the black mind. This inherent separation between the dominant and subaltern narrators is central to the contrast between traditional modes of narration and Faulkner's alternative poetics.

lumber mill. There, he catches a white man using loaded dice. This white man has been cheating the same group for years, but this time Rider attacks and kills the man. Importantly, Rider's actions are uncharacteristic. He does not react to the white man the way he has in the past, because he is consumed with grief.

This grief is not apparent when the sheriff's deputy relates the story to his wife. Instead, he says, "Them damn niggers [...] I swear to godfrey, it's a wonder we have as little trouble with them as we do. Because why? Because they aint human. They look like a man and they walk on their hind legs like a man, and they can talk and you can understand them and you think they are understanding you, at least now and then" (149). It is the deputy who is not understanding, however. As Rollyson says, "the deputy, like Zack, is caught in a system of prejudice he did not create, no matter how much his own actions may perpetuate it" (103). Aside from judgments of propriety and blame, the fundamental difference in the narration between Rider and the deputy ties this story to the others in the collection. The deputy tries to ascribe the murder as a definite cause and effect, a malady of the blood. The third-person narrator does not, opting instead for a fluid description of Rider's journey through grief.

"Go Down, Moses" also presents a fluid description of grief in the mourning of Mollie Worsham Beauchamp and her family. Gavin Stevens, the white attorney who also appeared at the end of *Light in August*, overhears this mourning and cannot cope with it. The Worshams grief is fluid, even melodic:

> "He dead," she said. "Pharaoh got him."
> "Oh yes, Lord," Worsham said, "Pharaoh got him."
> "Done sold my Benjamin," the old Negress said. "Sold him in Egypt."
> She began to sway faintly back and forth in the cair.
> "Oh yes, Lord," Worsham said. (361-2).

Stevens, feeling uncomfortable in the midst of this foreign grief, quickly leaves the house: "He descended the stairs, almost running. It was not far now" (362). He later apologizes for his grief to Mollie, who explains, "It's *our* grief" (363, emphasis mine). Gavin is not the racist deputy; he does not look at Mollie as less than human. In fact, he is one of the only people in the community who tries to help her. Despite this, her poetics so startles him that he is unable to interpret it.

Faulkner's poetics, then, ties all of these stories together, not Ike McCaslin. McCaslin is important in that he represents an inability to escape from a linear narrative, an inability shared by Quentin and Joe. He does, of course, form an alternate linear narrative than his peers, but he is still trapped. Despite this, nonlinear voices fill the novel with counterpoint. Robinson suggests these alternative voices are so strong that "History, here, becomes the history of blacks and women at the hands of white Southern men, a history perpetuated materially by bloodlines inscribed with previous rapes and betrayals" (197). I agree with Robinson that these voices are central to themes of the collection, but I also believe these voices give light, through contrast, to Ike's character.

Faulkner's alternative poetics is a framework through which we can understand his relationship to postcolonial criticism. Faulkner clearly represents the plight of subaltern characters, including white aristocrats. Quentin Compson struggles to find an identity for what he sees as his defeated country, ultimately being unable to do because he is unwilling to relinquish the dominant view of linear history. Similarly, Joe Christmas is robbed of an identity by confusing it with legitimacy. Ike, more fully than these other two characters, understands the way in which tying identity to legitimacy destroys the possibility of forming a fluid identity in the present. He recognizes in Sam Fathers what the people of Jefferson failed to recognize in Lena Grove. Despite his recognition, however, he still is tied to a linear narrative, concluding that everything is a part of God's plan.

While Faulkner's subaltern white characters never find a way to form an identity outside of the dominant ideology, Faulkner himself does display the type of poetics (what Glissant and Ladd call "creole poetics") that resists the dominant. Faulkner's narrative is fluid, not linear. He defers the event at Sutpen's Hundred until the very end. He tells the story of Joe Christmas out of chronological order, interchanging it with the stories of Hightower and Lena. Finally, he uses a series of sometimes only incidentally connected stories to explain Ike. Further, Faulkner allows other nonlinear voices to shine through his narration, a fact clearly seen in *Go Down, Moses*. In these narratives, Faulkner avoids co-opting the narration. He never enters the head of the characters, avoiding becoming Faulkner-in-Black-Face. Rather, he lets the voices stand alone. Such juxtaposition emphasizes the hybridity of the postcolonial South, offering a complex counterpoint of a variety of independent voices that stands in sharp contrast to the epic linear storyline of patrilineal History.

VI. Works Cited

Abdur-Rahman, Aliyyah I. "White Disavowal, Black Enfranchisement, and the Homoerotic in William Faulkner's *Light in August*." The Faulkner Journal 22 (2007): 176-92.

Aboul-Ela, Hosam. "The Political Economy of Southern Race: *Go Down, Moses*, Spatial Inequality and the Color Line." Quarterly: The Journal of Southern Culture 57 (2003): 55-64.

Ashcroft, Bill, Gareth Griffiths, and Helen Tiffin. The Empire Writes Back. London: Routledge, 1993.

Baker, Charles. William Faulkner's Postcolonial South. Ed. Yoshinobu Hakutani. Modern American Lit.: New Approaches 23. New York: Peter Lang, 2000.

Bleikasten, André. "Plots and Counterplots: The Structure of *Light in August*. Ed. Michael Millgate. New Essays on *Light in August*. The American Novel. Cambridge: Cambridge UP, 1987. 81-102.

Blotner, Joseph. Faulkner: A Biography. One-volume edition. New York: Chelsea House, 1986.

Bloom, Harold, ed. William Faulkner: Modern Critical Views. New York: Chelsea House, 1986.

Booker, M. Keith. A Practical Introduction to Literary Theory and Criticism. White Plains, NY: Longman Publishers, 1996.

Britton, Celia M. Edouard Glissant and Postcolonial Theory: Strategies of Language and Resistance. Charlottesville, VA: U of Virginia P, 1999.

Brooks, Cleanth. "Faulkner and the Muse of History." Mississippi Quarterly: The Journal of Southern Culture 28 (1975): 266-327.

Cobb, Michael. "Race and Religious Rhetoric in *Light in August*." boundary 2 32.3 (2005): 139-68.

Dabney, Louis M. The Indians of Yoknapatawpha: A Study in Literature and History. Baton Rouge: Louisiana State UP, 1974.

Doyle, Laura. "The Body against Itself in Faulkner's Phenomenology of Race." American Literature: A Journal of Literary History Criticism, and Bibliography 73.2 (2001): 339-64.

Duck, Leigh Anne. "Haunting Yoknapatawpha: Faulkner and Traumatic Memory." Faulkner in the Twenty-First Century: Faulkner and Yoknapatawpha, 2000. Ed. Robert Hamblin and Ann J. Abadie. Jackson, MS: UP of Mississippi, 2003. 89-106.

Dunn, Margaret M. "The Illusion of Freedom in *The Hamlet* and *Go Down, Moses*. American Literature 57.3 (1985): 407-23.

Faulkner, William. Absalom, Absalom!. New York: Vintage International, 1990.

---. Faulkner and the University. Ed. Frederick L. Gwynn and Joseph Blotner. Charlottesville: U of Virginia P, 1995.

---. Go Down, Moses. New York: Vintage International, 1970.

---. Light in August. New York: Vintage International, 1985.

Glissant, Edouard. Faulkner, Mississippi. Trans. Barbara Lewis and Thomas C. Spear. New York: Farrar, Straus and Giroux, 1999.

Godden, Richard. "*Absalom, Absalom!* Haiti, and the Labor Industry: Reading Unreadable Revolutions." William Faulkner's *Absalom, Absalom!*: A Casebook. Ed. Fred Hobson. New York: Oxford UP, 2003. 251-82.

Hamblin, Robert and Ann J. Abadie, ed. Faulkner in the Twenty-First Century: Faulkner and Yoknapatawpha, 2000. Jackson, MS: UP of Mississippi, 2003.

Hobson, Fred, ed. William Faulkner's *Absalom, Absalom!*: A Casebook. New York: Oxford UP, 2003.

Jackson, Chuck. "American Emergences: Whiteness, the National Guard, and *Light in August*." The Faulkner Journal 22 (2006): 193-208.

Klotz, Marvin. "Procrustean Revision in Faulkner's *Go Down, Moses*." American Literature 37.1 (1965): 1-16.

Lackey, Michael. "The Ideological Function of the God-Concept in Faulkner's *Light in August*," The Faulkner Journal 21 (2005): 66-90.

Ladd, Barbara. "'The Direction of the Howling': Nationalism and the Color Line in *Absalom, Absalom!*". William Faulkner's *Absalom, Absalom!*: A Casebook. Ed. Fred Hobson. New York: Oxford UP, 2003. 219-50.

---. "Faulkner Glissant, and Creole Poetics." Faulkner in the Twenty-First Century: Faulkner and Yoknapatawpha, 2000. Ed. Robert Hamblin and Ann J. Abadie. Jackson, MS: UP of Mississippi, 2003. 31-49.

Loichot, Valérie, "Glissant, Yoknapatawpha." Mississippi Quarterly: The Journal of Southern Culture 57 (2003): 99-111.

Long, Adam. "Religion as an Agent of Projection in *Light in August*." Philological Review 33.2 (2007): 51-66.

Millgate, Michael, ed. New Essays on *Light in August*. The American Novel. Cambridge: Cambridge UP, 1987.

Moore-Gilbert, Bart. Postcolonial Theory: Contexts, Practices, Politics. New York: Verso, 1997.

O'Donnell, Patrick. "Faulkner's Future Tense: A Critique of the Instant and the Continuum." Faulkner in the Twenty-First Century: Faulkner and Yoknapatawpha, 2000. Ed. Robert Hamblin and Ann J. Abadie. Jackson, MS: UP of Mississippi, 2003. 107-18.

Poirier, Richard. "The Bear." William Faulkner: Modern Critical Views. Ed. Harold Bloom. New York: Chelsea House, 1986. 48-62.

Reed, Joseph W., Jr. "*Light in August*." William Faulkner: Modern Critical Views. Ed. Harold Bloom. New York: Chelsea House, 1986. 63-92.

Robinson, David W. "'Who Dealt These Cards?': The Excluded Narrators of *Go Down, Moses*." Twentieth Century Literature: A Scholarly and Critical Journal 37.2 (1991): 192-206.

Rollyson, Carl E., Jr. Uses of the Past in the Novels of William Faulkner. Ann Arbor: UMI Research Press, 1984.

Said, Edward W. Orientalism. New York: Vintage Books, 1979.

Saldívar, Ramón. "Looking for a Master Plan: Faulkner, Paredes, and the Colonial and Postcolonial Subject." The Cambridge Companion to Faulkner. Ed. Philip M. Weinstein. New York: Cambridge UP, 1995. 96-120.

Spenko, James Leo. "The Death of Joe Christmas and the Power of Words." Twentieth Century Literature 28.3 (1982): 252-68.

Spivak, Gayatri Chakravorty. "Can the Subaltern Speak?". Williams, Patrick, and Laura Chrisman, eds. Colonial Discourse and Post-colonial Theory: A Reader. New York: Columbia UP, 1994. 66-111.

Stanich, Maritza. "The Hidden Caribbean Other in William Faulkner's *Absalom, Absalom!*: An Ideological Ancestry of U.S. Imperialism." Mississippi Quarterly: The Journal of Southern Culture 49.3 (1996): 603-17.

Taylor, Walter. Faulkner's Search for a South. Urbana: U of Illinois P, 1983.

Toomey, David. "The Human Heart in Conflict: *Light in August*'s Schizophrenic Narrator." Studies in the Novel 23.4 (1991): 425-69.

Trefzer, Annette. "Postcolonial Displacements in Faulkner's Indian Stories of the 1930s." Faulkner in the Twenty-First Century: Faulkner and Yoknapatawpha, 2000. Ed. Robert Hamblin and Ann J. Abadie. Jackson, MS: UP of Mississippi, 2003. 68-88.

Wadlington, Warwick. "Conclusion: The Stakes of Reading Faulkner—Discerning Reading." The Cambridge Companion to Faulkner. Ed. Philip M. Weinstein. New York: Cambridge UP, 1995. 197-220.

Weinstein, Philip M., ed. The Cambridge Companion to Faulkner. New York: Cambridge UP, 1995.

Winston, Jay S. "Going Native in Yoknapatawpha: Faulkner's Fragmented America and 'the Indian.'" The Faulkner Journal 18.1 (2002): 129-43.

Wittenberg, Judith Bryant. "Race in *Light in August*: Wordsymbols and Obverse Reflections. The Cambridge Companion to Faulkner. Ed. Philip M. Weinstein. New York: Cambridge UP, 1995. 146-67.

Zender, Karl F. "Faulkner and the Politics of Incest." American Literature 70.4 (1998): 739-65.

---. "Lucas Beauchamp's Choices." Faulkner in the Twenty-First Century: Faulkner and Yoknapatawpha, 2000. Ed. Robert Hamblin and Ann J. Abadie. Jackson, MS: UP of Mississippi, 2003. 119-36.

CPSIA information can be obtained at www.ICGtesting.com
Printed in the USA
BVOW06s2132300114

343519BV00008B/173/P